TEAMBUILDING STRATEGY

TEAMBUILDING STRATEGY

Mike Woodcock and Dave Francis

Gower

First published 1981 by Gower Publishing Limited as *Organisation Development through Teambuilding*. Second edition published by
Gower Publishing
Gower House
Croft Road
Aldershot
Hampshire GU11 3HR
England

Gower
Old Post Road
Brookfield
Vermont 05036
USA

Reprinted 1995

Mike Woodcock and Dave Francis have asserted their right under the Copyright, Designs and Patents Act 1988 to be identified as the authors of this work.

British Library Cataloguing in Publication Data
Woodcock, Mike
  Teambuilding Strategy. – 2Rev.ed
  I. Title II. Francis, Dave
  658.4
  ISBN 0–566–07496–6

Library of Congress Cataloging-in-Publication Data
Woodcock, Mike
  Teambuilding strategy/Mike Woodcock and Dave Francis.
    p. cm.
  ISBN 0–566–07496–6
  1. Work Groups. 2. Organizational effectiveness. I. Francis,
Dave. II. Title
HD66.W673 1994
658.4'02–dc20 93-48278 CIP

Typeset in 10pt Century Old Style by Poole Typesetting (Wessex) Limited and printed in Great Britain at the University Press, Cambridge.

Contents

List of Tables

List of Figures

Preface

As we move towards the 21st century, organisations are facing not only new opportunities but, also, greater threats. The changing centre of gravity of the economic world, moving from the West to the East, has brought many changes. Once comfortable, many Western organisations have seen their markets vanish as more industrious countries, particularly those around the Pacific rim, take over the mantle of 'workshop of the world'. But adversity is a shrewd teacher and we are now seeing some Western countries demonstrate that they can fight back and win. Underneath these observations lies a deeper question 'What does winning mean?' Is the industrial firm that plunders the Earth's scarce resources and degrades the environment really adding wealth for mankind? Perhaps we are entering an era when there will be a need to re-think the fundamental purposes of organisations.

Those who are responsible for the management of organisations are constantly seeking ways to be competitive, adaptable, innovative and productive despite all the environmental and competitive threats! As a result of many experiments, and billions of pounds expended by firms throughout the world, organisation development specialists have developed a set of theories about what constitutes a 'good' organisation and how to change a blocked organisation into one that is efficient and effective. Collectively these theories and associated interventions are known as 'Organisation Development' (OD).

When we review the experience of organisations around the world which have adopted the principles of OD – planned structural and cultural change – it is apparent that the results have been, at best, patchy. Some expensive errors have been made, many unfulfilled expectations generated and bold efforts have fizzled out when the commitment lessened. Organisation Development interventions have been tainted by those who have pursued enlightened goals which were discordant with the values of senior managers, failed to add value, or did not meet the operational needs of the organisation.

However, we have learned much from the application of the principles of Organisation Development. Especially significant was the realisation that many Japanese companies succeeded in incorporating the core OD values without adopting the formal processes of Organisation Development – suggesting that

OD is as much a state of the managerial mind as it is a series of planned and structured interventions.

One of the enduring themes of Organisation Development is the value of the team, which is seen as the 'fundamental building block' of organisation. Teams can be deliberately developed through the use of an integrated series of methodologies collectively known as 'team building interventions'. It would be wrong to claim that any collection of individuals can be developed into a close and effective team (imagine Hitler and Mother Teresa in the same group!) but the evidence suggests most people can be blended into a team providing that effective processes are used to facilitate group development.

Effective teamwork is a flexible organisational attribute. As military organisations have demonstrated all over the world, the 'fighting group' can cope with a vast range of challenges. For this reason teams are the core components of flexible organisations based on the hypothesis that fixed attributes are unable to provide the adaptive qualities needed by 20th century organisations. Rather an integrated set of organisational competences provides the framework for flexible advantage in uncertain times.

Effective teams bring the following benefits to organisations:

1. The individual is located within a meaningful group and so enjoys a sense of identity, recognition and fulfilment.
2. The team leader adopts an empowering and facilitating style which is progressive and acceptable when authoritarian models of management are less favoured.
3. Teams demand performance from their members and encourage people to give their best.
4. The multi-disciplinary nature of most teams increases the variety of problems that can be solved.
5. The variety of personality types adds quality to the decision making process.
6. The development of teams tends to de-emphasise the importance of hierarchy as more functions are undertaken at the work group level. This enables the removal of surplus layers thereby reducing management costs and removing potential communication blockages.
7. The use of information technology facilitates increasing devolution of decision making; down to the work group level. This allows senior management teams to operate both at the managerial and operational levels.
8. Teams permit the integration of individuals in relation to core values or generic programmes (for example, Total Quality Management).
9. Teams provide the social mechanism for aligning people behind a corporate vision.

These attributes of effective teamwork seem universally desirable but since the early research in the Hawthorne Works[1] it has been realised that teams can be a hostile social institution – at least as far as management is concerned. Teams have been shown to de-motivate, limit productivity and encourage the individual to achieve less than an acceptable performance. One of the authors recalls an early consulting experience when he studied a group of print workers who collectively agreed to produce about 25 per cent of a 'reasonable' level of output. Despite management's best endeavours over many years they never succeeded in breaking the team's power until new technology enabled every one of the workers to be dismissed and a new plant established with a completely new work force.

It is right, therefore, to conclude that team working, whilst widely desirable, is not a panacea. Those concerned with Human Resource Strategy cannot assume that teamwork is always needed and that teams are always positive. A much more cautious and strategic approach is appropriate. Hence this book.

We aim to help managers who are asking these questions:

1. What should be the focus of our management and organisation development interventions?
2. Should we undertake teambuilding initiatives?
3. How extensive should the teambuilding initiative be?
4. What resources will be necessary to support our teambuilding initiative?

The book provides the framework to answer such strategic HRD questions. We have striven to produce a structured, logical, coherent and organisationally relevant model to help those who are deciding 'should we do teambuilding?' The book is intended for senior managers, personnel and human resource specialists, team managers and consultants. As in our other books we aim to help practitioners who need a structured approach for analysis rather than an academic overview. For this reason you will not find an elaborate explanation of the considerable body of knowledge on teambuilding which now exists but a series of questionnaires and activities which will guide you through the key strategic decisions which should be taken by any organisation contemplating teambuilding.

Many readers will find it useful to have an overview of the structure of the book to help them navigate themselves to the most relevant sections without wasting time. The Introduction facilitates this and shows how an organisation development strategy incorporating teambuilding can be developed. Each later section answers key questions. By working through each of the stages in this book a broad strategy for teambuilding can be established for any organisation. In each section of the book an instrument is included as we find this to be the most convenient device for relating theory to practice. However, because organisations are complex it is impossible for a diagnostic instrument to always give full and complete data. Rather, the instruments provide the basis for enquiry: they are tools in the decision making process rather than substitutes for it.

This is the second edition of a book originally written in the early 1980s. At that time, although we were fervent believers in the value of teambuilding, we saw many organisations which had embraced teambuilding prematurely or were using team development technology with little lasting benefit. We believed that teambuilding should be strategically driven and organisationally appropriate if it was to give lasting benefit to the organisation.

Over a decade has passed and it is now time to reflect on our hypothesis that teambuilding is a powerful intervention into the life of an organisation but that it is not a universal tool to be used to solve all problems in all organisations. Reviewing the research evidence and examining another decade of consulting experience in hundreds of companies has not dented our belief that we were correct: we are still fervent believers in the value of teambuilding but we feel that organisations need to be ready to adopt this behavioural technology and must use teambuilding interventions judiciously. Teambuilding is not a fad but it should be used with caution and precision.

Second editions are always a delight for authors. All the foolish comments, under developed ideas and clumsy expressions which littered the first edition can be dealt with. The authors have the opportunity to write what they hoped to have written in the first place. However, this book is more than a simple re-edit. We have taken the opportunity to review the teambuilding research of the 1980s and 1990s, to reflect on our experience over that period and to bring our thinking up to date. Also, frankly, we are now much more experienced: over the past ten years we have conducted hundreds of teambuilding events as consultants and facilitators. We learn from each experience and, gradually, our expertise has developed.

The application of teambuilding techniques has mushroomed. Once an intervention for the experimentally minded, on the fringes of conventional management development practice, teambuilding has become an everyday happening. Today many managers hold 'away days' and teambuilding is used for many groups from shop floor workers to top executive teams. Indeed, some organisations are using teambuilding as the fundamental plank in the organisation development programme. This diversity of application of teambuilding technology has caused the authors to reflect on whether teambuilding is a unitary activity. We have come to the conclusion that these are real differences in the functional benefits, increasingly called 'deliverables', of different forms of teambuilding. Readers will find that we differentiate between different 'targets' of teambuilding in this edition much more precisely than in the first edition.

Management books tend to focus on the dominant issues of the time. Since the 1980s increasingly intense competition, reducing tolerance for inadequate performance and a decline in the competitive strength of the West, has brought harsher times for most managers. Teambuilding, indeed all organisation development interventions, needs to reflect this changing emphasis. They must provide mechanisms for finding and sustaining a competitive advantage (or capacity to add value in another way for non-commercial firms). The days when teambuilding was conducted by trainers who were trying to replicate the experience of the therapy group should be long gone. Although individuals themselves gain from being part of a close working group, teambuilding should be an organisation development intervention in pursuit of enhanced performance. Although it is true that individuals gain from being part of a close work group, we believe that the investment in teambuilding should clearly 'add value'.

Teambuilding, though important, is only one intervention in the chest of human resource development (HRD) tools. In the past two decades HRD people have begun to master the dynamics of managing substantial system change programmes. The growing sophistication of HRD tools means that the trainer has a greater variety of powerful interventions available. Teambuilding should be seen as just one of the change technologies available.

It is in this context that we began to produce this new edition. The task was challenging and we hope that the result makes a useful contribution to the growing body of literature to guide the HRD practitioner who should begin by asking the question not 'How should teambuilding be done?' but 'Should teambuilding be done at all?'

This book is dedicated to answering the second question. For this reason it is a strategic rather than an operational text. We hope that it will be directly useful to all those whose decisions shape organisation development strategy.

We are indebted to dozens of colleagues and hundreds of participants on our team building programmes some of whom have contributed to the ideas in the book. In particular we wish to thank Candy, our secretary, who ably prepared the text from our indecipherable handwriting.

NOTES

[1] Mayo, Elton, *The Social Problems of an Industrial Civilisation*, Routledge, London, 1975.

Mike Woodcock
Dave Francis

Introduction

Teambuilding has been one of the most enduring themes of organisation development over the past fifty years. In fact, Organisation Development grew from techniques of 'sensitivity training' which, somewhat crudely, demonstrated that people could learn to manage their transactions with others to achieve authenticity, energy and compassion. From such early experiments grew the realisation that organisational cultures could be shaped by providing focused experiences (later called interventions).

A *team* is defined as a group of people who must directly relate together to achieve shared objectives. By this definition not all groups are teams. Fifty people are not a team as they cannot relate directly together. Shared objectives are crucial: unless members have a common purpose there is no basis for teamwork. For example, a group of salesman each servicing a different geographical territory may be called a 'sales team'. However, by our definition they probably lack the necessary shared objectives and work individually. This sales group will not become a team until they are required to achieve a collective output by working together.

Teambuilding is a deliberate process of facilitating the evolution of a close and effective work group so that:

1. Team leadership is coherent, visionary and acceptable.
2. The team's roles, functions and 'deliverables' are clearly understood.
3. Members of the team have emotionally 'signed up' and dedicate their efforts to collective achievement.
4. There is a positive, energetic and empowering climate in the work group.
5. Meetings, both informal and formal, are efficient and make good use of time and available resources.
6. Weaknesses in team capability have been diagnosed and their negative effects mitigated or eliminated.

Teambuilding technologies focus on one or more of the six areas mentioned above. Teambuilding interventions are generally preceded by a diagnostic phase which identifies specific areas for improvement. When learning occurs within a team the benefits of new insights and improved skills can be readily applied.

1

Teambuilding interventions are centred on groups who work together in real life rather than a collection of individuals gathered for a training session. Unlike many training interventions teambuilding deals with real issues and has clear relevance to organisational objectives. Also, all the members of the team learn together; this creates a platform of shared experience which results in long lasting bonds. Team development occurs within the sub-culture of the group and, therefore, has an enduring and self-reinforcing quality. The implementation of learning is substantially increased by taking the team, rather than the individual, as the focus of an intervention.

The case for teambuilding is clear and potent. Many working groups contain excellent members yet fail to achieve even a passable level of efficiency. However, there are pitfalls for the unwary teambuilder. As teams are real working groups an intervention that goes sour can have serious and long lasting repercussions. It is possible to walk away from a training session held with strangers and say 'Well that was a real disaster and I hope that I'll never see any of those people again'. If the same reaction occurs to a teambuilding event the consequences are dire. Teambuilding demands high trainer skills and the significance of such events means that an experienced facilitator may be essential. Such experienced facilitators are rare and the scarcity of able resources undermines teambuilding as a strategy.

THE DEVELOPMENT OF ORGANISATIONS

There is so much complexity in organisations that it is difficult to generalise about the intent of organisation development. One organisation needs to become humanised, democratic and trusting, while another needs to become disciplined, task orientated and respectful of its leaders. It has been argued that every organisation tends to swing like a pendulum between opposites which are both desirable and undesirable at the same time! The conclusion must be that there are no universal prescriptive characteristics of an excellent organisation, there is no pot of gold at the end of the conceptual rainbow and the search for excellence yields diversity, not uniformity. Effective technologies for Organisation Development therefore begin with diagnosis. This has two principal dimensions: firstly transformational and, secondly, remedial. Let us explain what we mean by these terms.

Transformational organisation development is visionary in nature. The organisation changes its form, just as a chrysalis transforms into a butterfly. The essence of transformational change is the recognition that a diagnosis of the present situation will not yield the data necessary to design an appropriate series of developmental interventions, or bring about fundamentally needed change. It is necessary to re-explore the vision, develop a new strategic and structural intent and extrapolate the core competencies needed to transform the vision into a viable organisational form.

Remedial organisation development begins with the present and asks 'What is blocking us from being excellent in the here and now?' Many dimensions of organisational effectiveness are relevant: from culture to systems; from structure to resource management. The improvement of current operations (i.e. within the existing 'mind-set' of the organisation's power elite) can be a profound activity. The Japanese philosophy of Kaizen encapsulates this approach by recognising that many significant changes are the result of a myriad of incremental small improvements. In fact, the concentration on continuous development can lead to transformational changes as incremental changes accumulate into a critical 'mind-set' change. You will notice that we used the concept of 'blockages' to help explain remedial organisation development. We conceptualise organisations as multi-dimensional energy systems in which the flow of energy can become blocked or inhibited.

The six primary organisation development intervention levels available to the Organisation Developer are:

1. Intervening at the individual level to shape attitudes and enhance skills.
2. Intervening at the work group level to enhance group performance.
3. Intervening at the top team level to develop a strategically competent 'brain and heart of the firm'.
4. Intervening at the inter-team level to build supportive 'win–win' relationships between team members.
5. Intervening at the organisational level to improve structure, culture, systems or competencies.
6. Intervening at the external interface level to build a platform of support for the organisation with the various stakeholders whose opinions directly impact on the organisation.

For each of these six intervention level categories there is a set of 'tools' available. Some are specific to one level (for example, strategic management skill development is relevant only for level three) but others, especially teambuilding, are multi-use tools which are relevant at most levels. For example, one way of improving external interfaces (level six) is to bring together representatives of stakeholder groups and turn them into a team (albeit temporary) to explore the issues related to their roles and resolve the dilemmas caused by conflicts of interests.

Organisation development incorporates many techniques and frameworks. Many interventions are, at least in part, value-driven seeking, for example, to promote the principles of openness, commitment, participation, quality, empowerment and affiliation. Teambuilding techniques can support these core values but it is important that the style of facilitation used supports the underlying values which underpin a wider organisation development effort.

3

The most common errors when using teambuilding as an OD strategy appear to be:

1. Other, more important, organisational problems are ignored whilst teams are developed, leading to the accusation of 'fiddling while Rome burns'.
2. The prevailing organisational culture is hostile to the values of authenticity and openness which are a pre-condition for teambuilding.
3. Teams are unready to undertake a teambuilding process through lack of skills, inappropriate membership, inadequate resources, or because of past failures.
4. Teambuilding is unsuccessful because of a lack of sufficiently skilled internal or external facilitators.

These potential negative indicators provide us with the criteria to assess when teambuilding would be a productive intervention. We have found that team-building is an appropriate intervention only when:

1. The lack of effective teamwork is a serious 'blockage' to organisational effectiveness.
2. The organisational culture supports a team approach to getting things done.
3. Teams (especially team managers) are receptive and prepared to undertake the teambuilding process.
4. Adequate internal resources are available to aid teams through the team development process.
5. Internal resources are supported by external consultants who undertake difficult assignments and provide a professional counselling forum for internal staff.
6. Team managers and facilitators are aware of the 'technology' of teambuilding, in particular, the 'building blocks of effective teamwork'.

These six preconditions provide the structure for this book. In fact each can be phrased as a question. Answering the six questions will provide the organisational strategist with the necessary framework to decide 'is teambuilding the right intervention for us?'

The six questions are:

1. Is poor teamwork a significant organisational problem?
2. Does the organisation require a team approach?
3. Is the team ready for teambuilding?
4. Does the organisation have a resource of competent teambuilders?
5. Do we need external help?
6. What are the building blocks of effective teamwork?

The remainder of this book addresses these six questions, producing a conceptual framework for Human Resource Development strategists to determine the role that teambuilding should play in their organisation development priorities.

Part I: Is poor teamwork a significant organisational problem?

1 Organisational Effectiveness Areas

In this chapter we emphasise that teambuilding may be only one of a number of organisation development priorities and we present a conceptual model which permits the priorities to be assessed and ranked.

Of course, there are so many forms of organisation that any conceptual framework is bound to over-simplify a complex reality. However, the authors have found that the model presented is sufficiently broad to encourage an extensive review of organisation development priorities thereby reducing the risk that a solution is found before the problem has been fully identified.

You will find a simple instrument ('The Organisation Development Priorities Survey') in the following chapter. This is not a sociological research instrument, rather an interrogative checklist designed to raise consciousness about the range of possible organisation development needs.

Eight organisational issues are examined in The Organisational Development Priorities Survey. These are best expressed as the following questions:

1. Should we work to clarify our values, vision and aims?
2. Should we improve the quality of leadership to bring direction, alignment and attunement to the organisation?
3. Should we work on improving systems, methodologies and disciplines?
4. Should we develop a high energy climate which employees find satisfying, nurturing and stretching?
5. Should we develop the organisational structure so that it permits control and co-ordination which is appropriate for our range of task requirements?
6. Should we reform the power balance of the organisation to empower those lower down in the hierarchy?
7. Should we facilitate the fulfilment of individual aspirations and enrich the quality of life of each employee?
8. Should we develop teams so that groups become well motivated, share objectives and work together with efficiency and effectiveness.

Of course, these eight organisational priorities are not alternatives: in some cases several will need to be pursued in parallel. However, development resources are invariably limited and so organisation development strategists need to prioritise these effectiveness areas. It is better to progress one area to completion rather than dabble with three or four.

The survey instrument is relatively simplistic. This has the merit that only a few minutes are required to complete it. Hence, individuals should not feel that they are being disloyal as they complete the instrument. The output of the survey is a comparative assessment of the current strengths and development needs of the parts of the organisation under review. From this it is apparent that the survey can be used for an organisational unit: a site, business or primary function. Accordingly the survey manager should ensure that all informants share the same definition of the part of the organisation being reviewed.

We have mentioned the eight effectiveness areas and it is relevant to define them in more detail. However, we suggest that the material below is not shared with informants before they complete the Organisational Priorities Survey.

EFFECTIVENESS AREA ONE: CLEAR VISION, VALUES AND AIMS

The past decade has seen a resurgence of interest in the force within an organisation which brings vision, clarifies values and sets aims. Without vision the organisation operates without a 'head and a heart'. Since an organisation is a form of living entity – an organism – it needs, metaphorically, a 'brain' to give direction and a 'heart' to give meaning. Without a 'brain' and a 'heart' any organisation will fail to achieve its potential.

Clarity of vision, values and aims is the particular responsibility of the top management group who need to achieve a full consensus about ends and means. However, often the process is participative. There is a narrow gap between vision, values and aims. Conceptually values are the foundation and vision is the tangible expression of value fulfilment. From a vision aims must be distilled, to grasp a vision and transform it into an action plan. From here objectives can be set, tasks identified and success criteria established.

Although values endure, visions must evolve continuously as the wider environment changes. New opportunities and threats come bubbling to the surface and require evaluation and decision. As a general rule it is true to say that harsh or turbulent environments force organisations to set very clear goals and emphasise task orientated achievement.

Some organisations lack appropriate mechanisms for clarifying vision, values and aims. This results in unfocused effort, 'empire building' and low morale. Only when vision, values and aims are clear does the organisation possess the basis for alignment and attunement.

Key characteristics of a lack of vision, values and aims are:

1. There is significant doubt as to the core values of the organisation.
2. No coherent vision guides decision making in all parts of the organisation.

3. Members of the top management structure understand the vision in different ways and fail to support it in word and deed.
4. Different divisions and departments have not developed their missions within the context of the corporate vision.
5. Aims and objectives do not exist to transform the vision into reality.
6. Criteria for success are not clearly defined or comprehensively monitored.

When an organisation has a lack of vision, values or aims it requires an intervention to develop the strategic sense and integrity of the top management team. From this emerges the depth of consensus needed to give 'head' and 'heart' to the organisation.

EFFECTIVENESS AREA TWO: DYNAMIC LEADERSHIP

Leadership is the force within an organisation which mobilises human energy in pursuit of a vision. Leadership, therefore, is a human attribute which is re-invented from moment to moment. Unlike a values statement or a vision leadership exists in action – to borrow a phrase 'The medium is the message'. Not all leadership is effective or dynamic. Leaders have held organisations back and turned energy inwards and pursued a negative, insular vision.

Over the centuries many authorities, writers, managers and statesmen have tried to define the qualities of dynamic leadership. Some pundits emphasise human qualities like honesty, integrity, courage, positive dissatisfaction and self-confidence. Essentially leadership is an influencing process; so for every leader there must be at least one follower. Organisational Behavioural Scientists define leadership as 'meeting subordinates' needs for vision, support, and direction'. Leadership, therefore, is an individual capability directed towards collective achievement.

Just as management is hierarchical so leadership exists in levels. The supervisor of staff in the post room can exercise leadership; as can his boss, the divisional manager; and, of course, this is subsumed to the leadership of the top management group. We identify three primary levels of leadership within organisations which are shown in the diagram below.

A failure of leadership can occur at any of these three levels. If strategic leadership fails there is a lack of coherent aims, policies, decisions and resource allocation. If functional leadership fails there is a lack of specialised expertise and of a departmental voice at the top level. If task leadership fails there is a weakness of operational effectiveness so that things are neither done well nor sufficiently often.

Key characteristics of an organisation which shows a lack of leadership are:

1. The organisation lacks heroes and prophets.
2. Latent energy in people is not channelled into organisational achievement.

3. People in the organisation lack clarity about objectives, policies, standards, priorities and direction.
4. There is insufficient dynamism and an acceptance of the status quo.
5. People in the organisation feel there is no-one to look up to, which can lead to a lack of trust in the senior management group.
6. Individuals take initiatives which are not aligned towards a coherent set of organisational goals.
7. Challenges from the environment are underestimated or ignored.

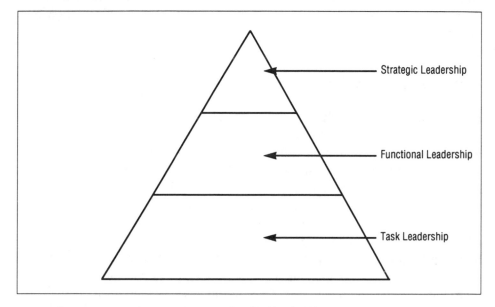

Fig. 1.1   Levels of Leadership

When an organisation suffers from a lack of leadership (at any of the three levels identified above) the remedies are largely individual. Sometimes training can be effective: people can learn to develop their leadership skills. Where this fails the remedy is change of personnel: since leadership is a human quality honed in youth the selection of 'natural leaders' is sometimes necessary to remedy an organisational resource weakness.

EFFECTIVENESS AREA THREE: VALUE-ADDING SYSTEMS

All organisations develop systems, methodologies, procedures and protocols. Such systems are essential for six key reasons:

1. Systems encapsulate organisational wisdom and prevent repetition of errors.
2. Systems enable complex events or processes to be co-ordinated and controlled.

3. Systems permit 'transparency' – they make it possible for supervision to be properly exercised.
4. Systems ensure reproductability – the same output can be achieved time after time.
5. Systems allow plans to be effected – without a solution many plans would be impotent.
6. Systems raise standards by reducing complexity and providing discipline.

Despite this impressive catalogue of advantages many people eschew systems giving them the pejorative label of 'mere bureaucracy'. It is true that formalisation and standardisation are traditionally thought to be intrinsic to systems, and so they impel the organisation towards uniformity (unless the systems design is focused on developing flexibility and adaptability – in a sense using systems to de-systemise the organisation).

The systems of an organisation can be likened to the systems of a human body. There are several key systems (the arterial, nervous, and so on) and many minor systems (sensory, chemical, and so on). The seven primary systems of an organisation give:

1. The control system: ensuring behaviour is kept within defined limits.
2. The planning system: creating the appropriate capabilities for future challenges.
3. The learning system: upgrading individual and collective competencies.
4. The task system: delivering outputs to superior quality, in sufficient numbers in a timely fashion.
5. The innovation system: creating products and services to be sold tomorrow.
6. The energising system: focusing and mobilising human energy to ensure a motivated organisation.
7. The sensing system: keeping open to significant stimuli in the internal and external environment.

Each system interlinks with others. Some organisational theorists use the model of electrons spinning around a nucleus to convey the discrete yet interdependent nature of these seven systems.

Under-developed, over-elaborated or wrongly focused systems cause degradation to the organisation. Some system inadequacies merely increase cost and blunt effectiveness. Other system failures are dire in their impact. We saw a flourishing business wither and disappear because the senior management team lacked essential information to control expenditure. Despite long hours of worry, members of the top team only discovered the depth of their financial horror when it was too late to remedy the situation. They blamed the lack of a financial and cost control system which led, as one manager forlornly remarked, to their 'setting to sea in a leaky boat'.

Key characteristics of weak or inappropriate systems are:

1. The inability of the organisation to codify learning.
2. Extensive administrative systems which do not add value.
3. Lack of organised integration between divisions and departments.
4. Top management lack the tools to understand the business.
5. Duplication of effort.

For an organisation with weak or inappropriate systems the remedies are expert intervention and task force projects. Most systems transcend organisational boundaries and so must be developed on an organisation-wide basis.

EFFECTIVENESS AREA FOUR: POSITIVE CLIMATE

The term 'organisational climate' is much debated. Everyone knows that organisations have a distinctive 'character' like a person, but organisational theorists who try to define the term are struggling to codify a complex and partly emotional reality. 'Culture' is best understood as 'organisational forces which shape employees' behaviour'. Many organisations lack a unitary culture: for example, the shop floor operates differently from the marketing department. Yet there is an overarching set of organisational forces which all employees recognise when they use the word 'we'.

Many of the forces which shape organisational culture are not under the direct control of management (although almost all can be influenced by management).

Organisational cultures develop to implement the organisation's strategy: for example, until the early 1990s Mercedes Benz fostered a culture of engineering excellence which led Mercedes Benz staff to support excellent engineering rather than market-orientated solutions.

Perhaps the most significant aspect of organisational culture is the way that power is allocated. Some organisations are hierarchical and formal whilst others are open and democratic. As democracy increases so 'empowerment' becomes a cultural characteristic and the institutions of participation are developed. Here much depends on the managerial philosophies of the organisation's leaders who shape the culture by their willingness to share real power.

Managers frequently ask the question 'is there any such thing as a positive climate?' The answer is 'Yes ...... and no!'. The characteristics of a positive climate are more stable than the requirements of organisational structure (see the next effectiveness area). All managements seek a climate which is energetic, demanding, task orientated and supportive of open communication. However, a distinctive culture is required for different tasks (a rock band requires a different culture from a Jesuit monastery) and organisation culture is affected by national culture (a Chinese corporation works on a very different principle from its American counterpart).

Developing a positive culture is a task that is difficult to grasp because managers lack both awareness and the levers for change. The task is made more difficult because many of the factors which shape culture are behavioural and symbolic: it is what powerful people do, not what they say, which really makes the difference.

Key characteristics of a negative climate are:

1. People do not make an energetic contribution to the organisation.
2. Fear and anxiety are widespread.
3. There is a lack of confidence and shared 'will to win'.
4. Destructive conflicts are common.
5. Too few people care about the well being of the organisation.
6. Loyalty is low or absent.
7. Information is not openly shared.
8. The culture fails to emphasise the key success factors for competitive advantage.
9. Top managers see the culture as a hindrance to their strategic plans rather than a help.

For an organisation with a negative culture the remedies are complex. Most important is the quality of leadership and it is frequently necessary for the senior management group to determine what are the behavioural characteristics of the culture they seek. Then comes the difficult step! Top managers must behave in ways that support and encourage the desired climate. Often other changes are required: the reward system (both formal and informal) needs to be redefined, a programme of indoctrination is often required and training can play a part. Most important, however, is the actual behaviour (and the messages this sends) of powerful people.

EFFECTIVENESS AREA FIVE: ENABLING STRUCTURE

All organisations (except perhaps those with fewer than four or five members) have a structure. The purpose of an organisational structure is to focus effort towards achievement. For very small organisations there is little choice – a 'boss' emerges who centralises authority and directs the organisation with a chosen degree of democratisation. In effect, in this 'simple structure' the control and co-ordination is effected in the mind of the boss.

With further organisational growth there are several available structural options. If the organisation's task is predictable and capable of being systematised then a mechanistic form develops. If the organisation's task is predictable but requires extensive individual skills then a professional form develops. If there are a range of different technologies or markets to focus on then the diversified form develops. To make organisation structure more complete there are

13

two other basic forms – the project or matrix organisation (sometimes called an 'adhocracy') and the decentralised organisation that is co-ordinated by a strong mission and is a 'values directed' form.

This brief analysis demonstrates that there is no such thing as a single best form of organisation. The type of organisation required is that which is suitable for the task (organisational sociologists call this 'contingency theory'). The four environmental contingency variables are these:

1. Degree of Environmental Predictability: the more predictable the environment the more mechanistic (rather than organic) the organisation becomes.
2. Degree of Autonomy Required by Operators: the more autonomy needed to adapt a body of expertise to individual situations the more decentralised the organisation becomes.
3. Degree of Multi-Disciplinary Effort required: the more multi-disciplinary effort needed the more the organisation forms around expert (often cross-functional) teams.
4. Degree of Management Commitment to Participative Organisational Models: the more committed are management to participation and empowerment the more devolvement of power, authority and responsibility will take place (selective decentralisation).

It follows that each management team must determine its own organisational form dependent on the environmental contingency factors mentioned above. There is no right answer – every organisational form has the weaknesses of its strengths. The aim is to come to the best answer bearing in mind that the availability of scarce talent is always a conditioning factor.

Key characteristics of an enabling structure are:

1. The structure inhibits task achievement.
2. Excessive resources are used.
3. Some parts of the organisation may be excessively flexible and adaptable and so lack discipline.
4. Some parts of the organisation may be inflexible and rigid so inhibiting change.
5. Power is strongest in areas which do not, directly, lead to the achievement of key organisational goals.
6. Tensions within the structure mean that managers are often blaming the organisational structure for poor performance and blockages.
7. It is difficult, or impossible, to recognise and resolve organisational problems.

The development of enabling structures requires an intervention which can address the 'fundamental architecture' of the enterprise. This can be done in two ways. Either a structural consultant is hired to give an expert and independent viewpoint or a task force is established to assess the problem and report to the senior executive group. Either way this is a topic which requires considerable expertise and the utilisation of specific analytical techniques.

EFFECTIVENESS AREA SIX: APPROPRIATE COMPETENCES

All organisations are facing a volatile and turbulent world. Since competition is now time based – it is getting there faster that pays dividends – conceptualising the business around standardised processes or activities has proven to be a weakness in some industries. It is much more effective to conceptualise a business on the basis of core competences as these can be opportunistically applied as new situations occur. Core competences give stability in an ever changing environment. For example, a firm may develop a core competence in total quality management which can be applied to all future projects and initiatives.

Core competences are not just resident in people's skills. They also exist in structures, systems, cultures and the accumulated resource capability of the organisation. For example a competence in customer service for a hotel requires top team commitment, staff training, specific system design, satisfaction measurement and budgeted customer service orientated projects.

Progressive organisations are conceptualising themselves as integrated 'families of competence' which link directly to their strategic vision. Basically the management process is straightforward. These are the key steps:

1. Clarifying the strategic vision and competitive strategy of the enterprise.
2. Identifying the world-class competences required to achieve the vision and competitive strategy.
3. Auditing current competences to find gaps.
4. Undertaking remedial, incremental and innovative competence development programmes to fill the gaps identified in step three.

The concept of an organisational competence is sometimes too 'soft' to be directly manageable. Precision of definition is achieved by setting sample performance and criteria (eg 80 per cent of all guests in the hotel should say that they prefer us to all of the other hotels in town). This allows a competence to become a managed programme. Such thinking has become especially well developed in the armed services. For example, a bomber squadron will seek to achieve the competence of rapid response and so will set targets for the time taken to get airborne, undertake repair schedules and so on. This enables the squadron managers to measure their performance and set management priorities.

Key characteristics of inappropriate competences are:

1. There are systemic weaknesses which continuously downgrade the organisation's performance.
2. Innovation is slower than that of competitors.
3. The organisation is not capable of delivering its planned strategy.
4. Excessive investment is targeted on areas which are incidental or irrelevant.
5. The organisation's capabilities are not coherent – they pull in different directions.

6. Important capabilities are not enhanced or developed.
7. Areas in which the organisation should be capable fail to be reflected in performance data.

Lack of appropriate competences requires an intervention to diagnose current strengths and weaknesses and establish the gap between the future and the 'now' situation. This can be analysed only when senior management become able to conceptualise the organisation as a system or family of integrated competences. The aim is to clarify the range of management initiatives needed to create the appropriate competences portfolio.

EFFECTIVENESS AREA SEVEN: DEVELOPED INDIVIDUALS

In the final analysis every organisation is only as strong as its people. This has many dimensions. The attributes needed by employees must be comprehensively defined. Effective methods of selection and training must permit the most able talent to be acquired and developed. Management of the processes of indoctrination and socialisation should shape the individual's attitudes and values so that there is a sufficient degree of intellectual standardisation and uniformity. Policies of empowerment should result in individuals feeling able to take initiatives and remedy organisational defects. Adoption of the principles of continuous self-directed learning will engender an openness and capacity to adapt which can transform people into sources of creativity and change. Every person needs to become a dynamic but positive component of the organisation.

Individual development is not a task solely for organisations but a partnership between the individual and the enterprise. In an earlier book[1] we identified eleven effectiveness areas for individual managers. These are:

1. Self management competence: being able to make the most of one's time, energy and skills. Being able to cope with the stresses of managerial life.
2. Clear personal values: having a set of values which have been deliberately chosen and provide a balance appropriate to working and personal life.
3. Clear personal goals: skilfully setting personal targets which facilitate self-development and meet material and career aspirations.
4. Continuous personal development: developing personal insight, ability and stature in order to rise to new challenges and opportunities.
5. Adequate problem-solving skills: having effective skills in individual and group problem-solving and decision-making.
6. High creativity: being able to generate new ideas and put them into practice.
7. High influence: making a significant impact on others; being listened to and gaining commitment to ideas and proposals.
8. Managerial insight: understanding the motivation of others and skilfully employing appropriate leadership styles and techniques.

9. High supervisory skills: having the practical ability to achieve results through organising the efforts of others.
10. High trainer capability: being able to help others to develop their skills, judgement, maturity and competence.
11. High teambuilding capacity: developing and using the potential of teams to achieve results unattainable by individuals.

Although managerial jobs differ from each other in the demands they make, each of these eleven effectiveness areas is potentially important to any manager. Improving individual performance begins for the manager with an analysis of strengths and weaknesses. Organisations can help create diagnostic and learning opportunities, although we believe that personal development is the ultimate responsibility of the individual.

Key characteristics of undeveloped individuals in an organisation are:

1. People in key jobs lack necessary ability.
2. Individuals fail to take responsibility for their own learning.
3. People do not match their skill development to that required by the organisation.
4. Latent abilities (which could be relevant to the organisation) remain underdeveloped.
5. Key skills are inadequately developed or missing.
6. People do not feel stretched by working for the organisation.
7. People become jaded because they lack a sense of personal excitement through self development.

Appropriate interventions for underdeveloped individuals include training but extend into all forms of job related learning including coaching, counselling, action learning and organisational redesign to facilitate individual development. It should not be forgotten that individual development requires a culture of respect for the person to facilitate the growth of the individual. Individual development takes place best in a culture that supports judicious risk taking.

EFFECTIVENESS AREA EIGHT: POSITIVE TEAMWORK

Ever since the Stone Age, when people gathered together in hunting bands to provide food for themselves and their families, men and women have found work teams a natural and resourceful way of getting things done. We see teamwork as a way of working in every area of life from a hospital operating theatre to an infantry unit.

Unfortunately, many teams fail to develop to their full potential as effective units. This largely results from team managers being unaware of the benefits of

17

teamwork and unskilled in the techniques of developing effective work groups. When a team is working well it is a highly resourceful, energetic unit which sustains individual morale and combines differing personal strengths into a powerful group. The word synergy describes this special blend of energy and competence.

An effective team will show the following characteristics:

1. It establishes and works towards clear objectives.
2. It has open relationships between members.
3. It grows stronger by sharing different viewpoints and gains from debate.
4. Members show a high level of support for each other.
5. Personal relationships are based on personal knowledge and trust.
6. People work together to get things done.
7. Potentially damaging conflicts are worked through and resolved.
8. Procedures and decision-making processes are effective.
9. Leadership is skilful and appropriate to the needs of the team.
10. It regularly reviews its operations and learns from experiences.
11. Individuals are developed and the team is capable of dealing with a variety of personalities.
12. Relations with other groups are co-operative and open.

The organisation which fails to develop the competence of its teams loses a vital resource. Organisations gain when managers are aware that their role is to convince everyone concerned of the value of teamwork and provide the necessary skills and support to enable teambuilding to take place.

Key characteristics of weak teamwork are:

1. Individuals lack a sense of affinity within their work groups.
2. There is insufficient co-ordination.
3. Teams become negative and 'anti-organisation'.
4. Informal communication is weak.
5. Trust and openness are lacking.
6. Teamwork is inefficient – things just do not get done.
7. Some team members fail to invest sufficient energy.
8. Teams fail to learn from experience and repeat mistakes time and time again.
9. Conflicts between team members fail to be resolved and sap energy.
10. The team's decision making processes are flawed.

Negative teamwork requires an intervention at the team level and teambuilding is appropriate. The aim is to bring together the members of the team and transform them into a close, effective and positive work group which achieves tasks within the context of the organisation's vision and goals.

This chapter has argued that there are eight generic organisation development needs which are interdependent but are conceptually distinct. These are shown in the diagram below.

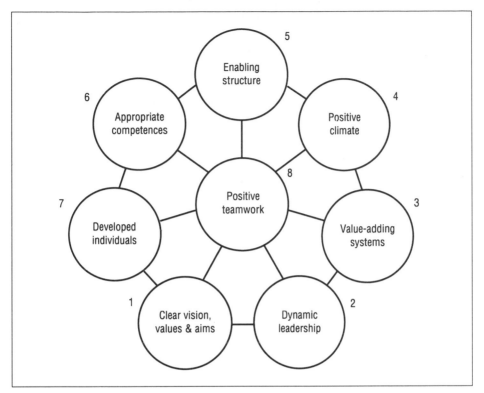

Fig. 1.2 The Organisational Effectiveness Model

The main thesis of this chapter has been that organisation development interventions need to be focused on the specific requirements of the organisation at a point in time. Only if there is a lack of positive teamwork should this be the primary organisation development programme. Although the other seven organisation development needs may incorporate team building, the thrust needs to be aimed at solving the real issues. Strategic development of organisations begins with a thorough diagnosis to identify which of the eight areas is a priority.

NOTES

[1] Woodcock, M. and Francis, D., *The Unblocked Manager*, Gower, Aldershot, 1982

2 The Organisation Development Priorities Survey

To assess whether the development of effective teamwork is a priority for an organisation it is necessary to answer the broader question 'What development needs does the organisation have at this time?'

The Organisation Development Priorities Survey helps to do this by collecting opinions, clarifying options and assisting senior management to evaluate 'the state of the nation'.

When using the survey it is important to work within the following guidelines:

1. Obtain as wide a spread of input as possible.
2. Beware of increasing expectations and then frustrating them.
3. Provoke discussion about the results in order to validate them.
4. Consider the results as indications rather than as scientific facts.
5. Influence those with organisational power to consider seriously the findings.
6. Move towards action rather than repeated diagnosis.
7. Re-evaluate from time to time.

THE SURVEY – HOW IT IS CONSTRUCTED

The survey is in two parts. The first part is used for the collection of data, and the second part, which may or may not be used with respondents, provides an explanation of the outcomes. The survey uses a points allocation design. This has the advantage that all of the key areas are compared with each other so that a comparative priority is established. However, the survey design does not indicate the magnitude of problems and senior managers will need to take the final decision as to where decisive action is needed.

In completing the survey respondents are asked to allocate 10 points to each of six parts and it is important that a briefing is given which emphasises that the survey is designed to identify priorities and that whilst choices are often difficult they are necessary if the organisation's development resources are to be used wisely.

HOW TO USE THE SURVEY

The survey asks managers and others with a viewpoint on the organisation to record their views. It takes people about ten or fifteen minutes to complete the survey. It is important that the process of data collection is managed carefully as simple errors in procedure can invalidate the results. We suggest that the following steps are taken:

Step One

Define the part of the organisation you wish to survey. This may be a department, function, site, project group, company or the total organisation. It is essential that everyone completing the survey is considering the same 'unit' and this should be clearly stated on the front of the survey form. People should be asked to survey only those parts of the organisation with which they have personal experience.

Step Two

Prepare a briefing statement which states the purpose of the survey and describes the uses to which the data will be put. It is important to ask for truthful views and to try to ensure that unwarranted expectations are not aroused.

Step Three

Collect viewpoints from a broad and representative sample of informants. Different levels within the hierarchy usually have distinct viewpoints and it is important that all perspectives are represented. Some organisations may choose to collect data anonymously.

Step Four

Ensure that those responsible for change need to work through the results in detail. Action is usually stimulated by a deep review and discussion.

Step Five

Use the survey from time to time to review progress. A periodic assessment is a valuable tool in monitoring progress.

Step Six

Decide whether the survey will be scored by the respondent or by someone centrally. When self scoring is used the respondent is issued with Parts One and Two. When central scoring is used the respondent is issued only with Part One.

ORGANISATION DEVELOPMENT PRIORITIES SURVEY – PART ONE

This survey invites you to review your organisation and help to strengthen it in the future.

The first step is to be clear about which part of the organisation you are considering. You may be surveying a department, function, site, company or total enterprise. If the box below is not already completed write a definition of that part of the organisation in the space below; we will call it the *unit*.

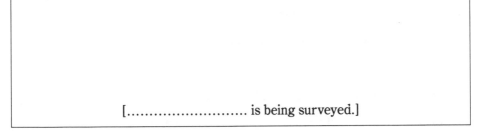

[.......................... is being surveyed.]

In respect of the unit described above *only*, consider each of the sections below.

Please take great care to understand the scoring system before you begin! Ask if you are unsure.

The Questionnaire contains six sections, each of which should be considered separately. For *each* section you have 10 points to allocate. The number of points given for any statement should reflect the extent you perceive that characteristic is present in the organisation. The more strongly a particular attribute is present the more points should be allocated.

You must allocate 10 points – no more, no less – for each section.

SECTION ONE

Consider the statement below. You have 10 points to allocate. The number of points given for each item should reflect the extent you perceive that characteristic is present in the organisation.

Many people who work in this organisation might be overheard saying...

POINTS

1. 'I am 100% clear where the organisation is heading' _____

2. 'those who are leading the organisation are doing a first rate job' _____

3. 'our systems are effective and efficient' _____

4. 'everyone wants to work' _____

5. 'this organisation is "well organised"' _____

23

6. 'people have the right skills to do their jobs'   _____

7. 'people get a good chance to develop their potential here'   _____

8. 'almost everyone feels "really part of the team"'   _____

SECTION TWO

Consider the statement below. You have 10 points to allocate. The number of points given for each item should reflect the extent you perceive that characteristic is present in the organisation.

I like working for this organisation because...

                                                                                                                        POINTS

9. The organisational structure enables me to get things done   _____

10. Effective systems make it possible to stay on top of the job   _____

11. I feel part of an organisation with a strong vision   _____

12. People work together very positively   _____

13. I have enjoyed a great deal of personal development   _____

14. I respect those in charge   _____

15. Things get done properly   _____

16. There is a great deal of positive energy around here   _____

SECTION THREE

Consider the statement below. You have 10 points to allocate. The number of points given for each item should reflect the extent you perceive that characteristic is present in the organisation.

The real strengths of this organisation are...

                                                                                                                        POINTS

17. People are capable and responsible   _____

18. Destructive 'politics' are absent   _____

19. Top managers are excellent leaders   _____

20. There is a clear strategy for the future   _____

21. Teamwork is widely practised   _____

22. Systems provide information when it is needed   _____

23. Decisions are taken at the right level   _____

24. The organisation is good at 'getting things done'   _____

SECTION FOUR

Consider the statement below. You have 10 points to allocate. The number of points given for each item should reflect the extent you perceive that characteristic is present in the organisation.

If there is a crisis...

                                                            POINTS

25. Top managers effectively take charge   _____

26. Teams get together to solve problems   _____

27. The organisation just copes effectively   _____

28. Individuals take vigorous initiatives   _____

29. Everyone invests extra energy   _____

30. Clear objectives are set to overcome the crisis   _____

31. Systems can deal with unexpected difficulties   _____

32. People have been trained to manage in a crisis   _____

SECTION FIVE

Consider the statement below. You have 10 points to allocate. The number of points given for each item should reflect the extent you perceive that characteristic is present in the organisation.

A great deal of time and money has been invested in...

                                                            POINTS

33. Getting people to work well in teams   _____

34. Developing the talents of individuals   _____

35. Ensuring that motivation is high   _____

36. Using the benefits of Information Technology   _____

37. Communicating vision and strategy downwards   _____

38. Ensuring that the organisation's structure is effective   _____

39. Developing the most senior managers   _____

40. 'Benchmarking' ourselves against the world's best   _____

SECTION SIX

Consider the statement below. You have 10 points to allocate. The number of points given for each item should reflect the extent you perceive that characteristic is present in the organisation.

Compared with competitors we are...

POINTS

41. Faster and more capable   _____

42. Clearer about the future   _____

43. Better organised   _____

44. Strongly led by able people   _____

45. Helped by efficient systems   _____

46. Open, energetic and positive   _____

47. Organised in dynamic teams   _____

48. Resourced with talented individuals   _____

ORGANISATION DEVELOPMENT PRIORITIES SURVEY – PART TWO

SCORING THE SURVEY

Instructions

Copy your scores for each question below. When you have done this, add your scores horizontally. Then read the explanations of the organisation development priorities.

INTERPRETING THE RESULTS

After scoring, each of the eight factors will have a score of between 0 and 60. The lower scores indicate organisational problems and are likely to be priorities for a

Question Numbers						Your Totals	Area
1	11	20	30	37	42		VVA
2	14	19	25	39	44		DL
3	10	22	31	36	45		VAS
4	16	18	29	35	46		PC
5	9	23	32	38	43		ES
6	15	24	27	40	41		AC
7	13	17	28	34	48		DI
8	12	21	26	33	47		PT

Table 2.1 Survey Scoring Chart

programme of planned change. Higher scores represent organisational strengths. The scoring sheet included here enables an individual to complete the survey and interpret his or her personal result. Where the survey is completed across a team, the data can be further analysed using the suggested format given below.

EXPLANATION OF RESULTS

The questionnaire examined eight areas of organisational effectiveness in order to provide a basis for discussion and ultimately for establishing priorities for further development.

You have now analysed the results of the Organisational Development Priorities Survey and obtained a comparative assessment of the strengths and weaknesses of the unit in relation to the eight effectiveness factors described below. A low score in any area suggests that it could be a priority area for development. Here is a description of the eight effectiveness factors.

1 Clear vision, values and aims

Top managers have carefully defined the organisation's vision, values and aims and ensured that these are well communicated throughout. Individual managers relate their work to corporate goals and people clearly understand the mission

27

of the organisation. There is a set of development aims which take the organisation forward.

2   Dynamic leadership

Those in managerial positions adopt an assertive and vigorous approach and take a positive leadership role. They adopt an approach which emphasises achievement and problem solving. People look up to their leaders and trust them to take sound decisions.

3   Value-adding systems

Systems and procedures are carefully designed to provide control without inhibiting initiative or flexibility. They enhance rather than inhibit the effectiveness of the organisation. The benefits of Information Technology are used to increase control, but this may be delegated to lower levels. Each system improves the quality of decision making.

4   Positive climate

Attitudes and relationships are, on balance, friendly, co-operative, open and positive. People make efforts to help each other and support the organisation in achieving its objectives. There is a spirit of energy and confidence. Trust is high and there is a 'we can do it' spirit.

5   Enabling structure

The hierarchical structure of the organisation is suitable to the tasks being completed and enables work to be effectively completed. Large organisations are broken down into smaller units. The organisational structure facilitates the processes which add value.

6   Appropriate competences

A competence is the capability to achieve to world class standards. The organisation has the capabilities needed to transform its strategy into action. This includes competences not only of people, but also of systems, technologies, resources and facilities.

7   Developed individuals

People have skills to perform their current jobs to a world class standard and their individual potential is developed. They participate in their own learning and the organisation adapts continuously as skills are enhanced.

8   Positive teamwork

People work well together and team resources are co-ordinated effectively. Meetings achieve useful results and projects are accomplished effectively. All teams have appropriate leadership, balanced membership, effective work methods, positive climate and clarity about their role within the wider organisation.

Following your analysis you are in a better position to decide on eight key questions:

1. Should we work on our definition of vision, values and aims?
   and/or
2. Should we emphasise the development of effective and assertive leadership?
   and/or
3. Should we upgrade our information technology, management processes, control systems and communication procedures?
   and/or
4. Should we develop a more positive organisational climate characterised by openness and high energy?
   and/or
5. Should we change our management structure so that it is 'fit for purpose'?
   and/or
6. Should we develop new organisational competences?
   and/or
7. Should we emphasise personal, job and career development for individuals?
   and/or
8. Should we improve our teamwork?

Part II: Does the organisation require a team approach?

3 Key Teams and their Effectiveness

Some organisations are more team orientated than others. For example, a major public utility company in Hong Kong has abandoned the notion of asking some individuals to set personal objectives and asks each team to set group aims and targets. Each team manager is trained as a team leader and describes himself as a 'facilitator'. Conversely, some organisations have gone the other way, seeing teamworking as a human relations fad which undermines the concept that every individual is responsible for a defined set of tasks. In such organisations managers argue that if everyone is responsible then no one is responsible.

To some extent the culture towards teambuilding is based on whether managers have been predominantly influenced from the East or the West. Much Eastern management thinking is based on the principle that the individual functions best within a close, supportive yet demanding 'family group'. In the West there has been a different trend: individualism, personal strength and difference are prized. Both theories have their success stories but are very different in application.

The team approach thrives in a management culture which:

- values the power of the team
- sees objectives (at least in part) as collective
- de-emphasises competition between individuals
- emphasises the benefit of synergy and inter-dependency
- is willing to put resources into team building
- accepts that some tasks are performed better by work groups rather than individuals
- defines the role of the supervisor as a team leader
- supports the notion that one person's weaknesses are compensated by another's strengths

Of course, sometimes a team-orientated culture makes sense. Consider a crew unloading a truck and moving the contents into a warehouse. Clearly this is a team task: much of the success of the unloading crew is a function of the degree to which they succeed in working together co-operatively. But should one apply the same logic to a group of salespeople selling vacuum cleaners door-to-door?

Here each salesperson has his or her territory, they compete for bonuses and hardly interact at all. It can be argued that, in such sales organisations, a team ethos would be counterproductive as it undermines the principle of aggressive individuality which is the key motivator of vacuum cleaner salespeople.

We conclude that organisations cannot be treated as single entities culturally: after all a firm may have both sales staff and unloading crews. Each part needs a distinct cultural identity which promotes its key tasks within a broad cultural framework of the parent organisation. This is possible: Paris and Nice each have a very distinct culture yet they are both French cities!

Strategic teambuilding requires key teams (i.e. 'suitable cases for treatment') to be identified, their current level of team development needs to be assessed and needed team competencies clarified. In this chapter we work step-by-step through these three issues.

IDENTIFYING KEY TEAMS

Most organisations can be conceptualised as an interrelated set of teams (in fact, it is a powerful exercise to draw the organisation chart based on the assumption that teams, not individuals, are the real building blocks). It is useful to define teams by their functionality. In many organisations we recognise six primary types of team. These are:

1. Strategic teams: Responsible for determining strategy, core values, policies, structure, resource allocation and integration.
2. Management teams: Groups of managers responsible for a distinct technology or work area.
3. Project teams: Temporary teams formed to accomplish time bounded tasks.
4. Co-ordination teams: Part-time groups which manage interfaces and co-ordinate complex tasks.
5. 'Think–tank' teams: Groups which act as catalysts and supporters of decision making (may be full or part time).
6. Work groups: Teams which complete the core tasks of the organisation.

Such teams do not have exclusive membership. One person may be a member of several teams, whose boundaries may be fluid and indistinct.

NEED FOR TEAMWORK

Our definition of the importance of teamwork is based on the 'teamwork index' which is a 'rough' but effective way of defining whether a team has a significant teambuilding requirement. The teambuilding index is based on two dimensions: the importance of effective performance and the degree of interdependence between team members. Each team is given a teamwork index expressed as a percentage. The table below identifies six categories.

Need Rating	Team Characteristics
100 per cent	A highly independent team which has to perform well to meet the requirements of the organisation. Poor team performance increases the risk of extreme damage to the organisation's image, functioning or performance
80 per cent	A team in which all members must work together well although each member has distinct areas of responsibility. Low team performance could have a severe but not catastrophic impact
60 per cent	An important team but not one that is crucial to organisational performance. Each member has personal objectives but there are considerable needs for communication, co-ordination and shared activities. It is important that co-operation is maintained
40 per cent	An important group that sometimes works as a team but more often members operate independently or with a few of the others. Some needs for co-ordination and communication but few shared activities. Co-operation is desirable
20 per cent	A loose grouping of individuals whose work overlaps or who need collective motivation. There is little, if any, interdependence but members may learn from each other's experience
0 per cent	Not a team in fact (although perhaps in name). Members work independently with no requirement to co-operate

Table 3.1 Teamwork Index Table

Clearly, teambuilding efforts should be concentrated on those teams which have a high teamwork index. The further an organisation extends teambuilding to teams with lower index scores the more it is operating a policy that teambuilding is a 'nice to have' experience rather than a 'must have' experience.

Do all teams with an index of 60 per cent or higher need teambuilding? The answer is 'no' – because some teams with a substantial requirement already function as effective teams. Accordingly we need a framework to assess the current stage of team development of each key team. This we will complete in the next section of this step. It is then possible to determine the teambuilding needs, team by team, using the following logic:

- Low team index and low development stage = low teambuilding need
- High team index and low development stage = high teambuilding need
- Low team index and high development stage = low teambuilding need
- High team index and high development stage = moderate teambuilding need

The last statement requires some explanation. Teams with a high team index and a high current development stage need to keep renewing their team capability or it may degenerate: hence we classify the need as 'moderate'. The argument is that a person may be a good tennis player but continued prowess requires continued learning.

TEAM EFFECTIVENESS

Team effectiveness is best assessed against a standardised model for the purpose of classification. We use a six stage model of team development described below. Later you will identify the current stage of development of each key team which provides both an element in the assessment of teambuilding needs and brings clarity as to the correct focus for any proposed teambuilding intervention (the aim of which is to help the team move to a higher state of development).

Teams almost invariably develop through a series of stages as they progress from an immature collection of individuals to a closely integrated and effective working group. During this period procedures, methods of operation and team climate undergo tremendous changes.

Any attempt at defining these stages, and the changes associated with them, must be an over-simplification. However, we have found that a straightforward model based on six stages of development is very useful in helping to review organisational teams and determine which are likely to be the most receptive to change.

The principle we utilise is this: if a team needs to work effectively but is inhibited from doing so by being at too low a stage of development, then it is ripe for teambuilding investment.

Teams need to be categorised on the six stage model (Teamwork Index Table). Evaluations will necessarily be somewhat 'broad brush'; however, the purpose is to conduct a broad assessment; a detailed study of team functioning will be conducted later.

Here is our description of the six stages of team development.

STAGE A: 'RITUAL' SNIFFING

Whenever animals come together there is a period of testing out and getting acquainted. A similar process exists when new teams are formed. People seek to identify their place in relation to others. One characteristic of teams at this stage is that feelings and genuine emotional reactions are usually hidden. People tend to conform to the established line, partly because they are apprehensive. The person in a formal position of authority is central, and people watch to see how he or she behaves.

Meetings often consist of a series of statements with team members queueing to put their point of view without listening to what goes before or afterwards. Often little care is shown towards other people or their views and that is frequently characterised by a lot of talking and little real listening. Personal weaknesses tend to be covered up because the group lacks the skill to support team members. Mistakes may be used as 'evidence' to help convict people rather than as opportunities to learn. There is often only a shallow understanding of what needs to be done as objectives are poorly set and communicated.

Politeness and order are the best that can be expected at this stage. However, this condition is only skin-deep. Difficulties related to inadequate procedures, inter-personal difficulties and uncertain commitment lurk, like minefields, waiting to 'blow up'. This tends to occur in Stage B.

STAGE B: 'INFIGHTING'

As the team develops it becomes important to differentiate personal relationships and clarify power and authority relationships. The team manager has particular status because his or her position has been recognised by the organisation and the trappings of influence have been allocated to the role. Yet this position has to be earned. Team members carefully watch and evaluate their manager's performance. They may accept leadership gladly or find cunning ways to avoid it.

Relationships between team members become more significant at this stage. Alliances are forged and cliques often form. Certain individuals become liked and respected by others. Other people find that their colleagues are irritating or unacceptable. Animosities, expressed more or less politely, rise to the surface. Commitment by members to the work of the team is often a key issue. Some individuals may use the group for ulterior motives, with some devious personal strategy underlying apparently civilised behaviour.

Teams comprising both men and women are especially interesting at this stage. Elements of sexual competitiveness are sometimes present. People compete for attention and wish to be seen as especially attractive or powerful. Sex is an extremely energising and motivating force in many teams and organisations and issues of sexual attraction, repulsion or indifference may need to be worked through.

Development through the infighting stage occurs with deeper inter-personal knowledge and the building of a group climate which enables people to express their differences and find common understanding. The integrity and overall unity of the team becomes more important than individual gratification.

STAGE C: 'EXPERIMENTATION'

This stage begins when the team decides that it wishes to review seriously its operating methods and undertake activities to improve its performance. The team becomes willing to experiment; to sail in 'uncharted waters'. Problems are more openly faced and the underlying values and assumptions affecting decisions begin to be debated. More risky issues are opened up and often the way the group is managed is an early topic for discussion. Personal issues are raised, feelings respected and personal animosities dealt with. This may lead to some traumatic encounters between team members, but the quality of their relationship is now sufficient to support individuals through such upheavals.

The team becomes more inward-looking, and for a time may reject other individuals or groups. This is a transient phase in which the energy of the group is devoted to solving its own problems of relationship and effectiveness. The quality of listening undergoes marked improvement. Functioning within the team can become uncomfortable but also dynamic and exciting.

However, the team still lacks the capacity to function in an economical, unified and methodical way. Some inter-personal issues have been resolved and there is a climate which supports individuals and gives energy to the next stage – the search for effectiveness.

STAGE D: 'EFFECTIVENESS'

The team now has the confidence, open approach and trust to examine its operating methods. Generally the team now needs to look at the procedures and problem-solving skills it uses to conduct its business. These have to be reviewed in substantial depth. Each person in the team needs to contribute to developing the processes to be used. Frequent review is required to provide the data for improving effectiveness.

The work of the team becomes identified with precision, contributions are clarified and improved and clear objectives are set. Team members become concerned with economy of effort and task effectiveness. The team becomes more competent to handle problems creatively, flexibly and effectively. This stage is vital because without this attention to its working methods the team will continue to use marginally effective modes of operation and satisfy itself with an adequate performance, rather than striving for excellence.

As the team develops through this stage, it becomes genuinely proud of its capacity to perform and achieve. Results improve and recognition comes from other sources. Team members value their involvement more, protecting the team from threats to its well-being. The team grows in competence and resourcefulness. Membership takes on a real significance for everyone concerned at the next stage – maturity – is reached.

38

STAGE E: 'MATURITY'

By now the team has achieved the openness, concern and improved relation-ships of Stage C and the effective working methods of Stage D. Maturity means that the team can develop open relationships with other groups and flexibility becomes the keynote. Processes and procedures are adopted to meet different needs, leadership is decided by the situation and not by protocol. The group itself recognises the kind of leadership which is necessary for the challenge being faced and the leader recognises the need to involve the team in matters of substance. Everyone's energies are utilised for the benefit of the team. There is a strong sense of pride in the achievements and a satisfying relationship devel-ops between members. However, each individual's needs are met as the team is genuinely concerned with the well-being of each person.

The team is responsive and responsible as it considers basic issues and the human aspects of decisions. It realises that it is part of a larger organisation and has moral responsibilities. Trust and openness, co-operation, confrontation and a continual review of results become part of the way of life. The desire to develop means that competent outside help is welcomed.

The team is not only admired, but it is emulated by others. Roles of individuals are clear and each person's contribution is important and distinctive. A mature team does not allow its function to become redundant or obscure; it influences others to give recognition and support.

STAGE F: 'DEGENERATION'

Some teams pass beyond the 'maturity' stage and go into decline. There is a 'tiredness' and a 'sameness' about the team that makes it dysfunctional. Ideas dry up, complacency sets in and all the members of the team begin to think alike (this has been called 'groupthink'[1]). The degeneration stage can lead to the team making decisions which are unrealistic, insular and irrational: outside inputs are ignored and team members who express divergent views are 'removed'.

The degeneration stage often follows a successful period of teambuilding. Ironically, the stronger the team the more likely it is to enter a degenerative phase. From the success of teamworking comes a feeling of self satisfaction which allows the team to become complacent and inward-looking.

Not all teams enter this degenerative phase – some continue to function well for many years. However, teambuilders cannot afford to assume that a strong team will always remain capable – continued questioning and openness is required.

NOTES

[1] Janis, I.L., *Groupthink: Psychological Studies of Policy Decisions*, Houghton Mufflin, Boston, 1982.

4 The Teambuilding Priorities Assessment

This chapter takes the ideas explored in the previous section and develops a structured process for identifying key teams, assessing each team's requirement for teambuilding (the 'teambuilding index') and each team's stage of team development.

The process is designed to help you decide where to begin in a teambuilding programme. Chapter Three provides the theoretical basis for the approach. Here is an overview of the process:

Step One	Key Team Identification. In this step you are asked to list all the key teams in the organisation.
Step Two	Assess the requirement for teambuilding using the team index.
Step Three	Assess the current stage of development of each key team by identifying which of the six stages of team development best represent the current capability of the team.
Step Four	You now have a list of key teams, an assessment of the importance of effective teamwork and an assessment of the stage of team development. Armed with this you can highlight those teams which require a teambuilding intervention.

STEP ONE

List all the teams in your organisation on the work sheet. Assign each of the teams to one of the six categories as indicated then indicate those teams with a * that you wish to assess. Carry a list of the * teams forward to step two.

DOES THE ORGANISATION REQUIRE A TEAM APPROACH?

Work Groups	Think Tank Teams	Co-ordination Teams	Project Teams	Management Teams	Strategic Teams

Fig. 4.1   Key Team Development Worksheet

STEP TWO IMPORTANCE OF TEAM EFFECTIVENESS

Assign a team index using the Teamwork Index Table from Chapter Three page 35. This should be expressed as a percentage and should be completed for each team separately. The team index categories can be summarised as:

Vital Importance High Interdependency	Medium Importance Significant Interdependency	Low Importance Low Interdependency
100 % 80 %	60 % 40 %	20 % 0 %
Team Building Essential	Team Building Desirable	Team Building Irrelevant

STEP THREE STAGES OF TEAM DEVELOPMENT

Assess the current state of team development by deciding which of the six stages best represents the current development stage of each key team. Refer to the behavioural descriptions of the team development stages overleaf to assign each team a letter between A and F. This is a question of judgement. Only consider teams with a 40 per cent or higher team index from Step Two ('the threshold teams'). Record your decisions on the table in Step 4 (page 44).

STEP FOUR TEAMBUILDING PRIORITIES WORKSHEET

Bring forward the list of key teams with a medium to high team index score to the worksheet overleaf. Add the team development stage (a letter between A and F). Then determine a priority for teambuilding on a 10 point scale in the last column. In principle, teams with a high priority (high team index scores) who have not reached stage D or E (or who have entered stage F) are priority cases for a teambuilding intervention.

DOES THE ORGANISATION REQUIRE A TEAM APPROACH?

Key Teams (list from Step One)	Teamwork Index %

Fig. 4.2 Teamwork Significance Work Sheet

Insular thinking Low energy Complacency Absence of creative conflict Orthodox thinking Superiority syndrome Lack of outward challenge Tiredness shows Groupthink sets in Unrealistic, insular and irrational decision making Divergence not tolerated		**Stage F** **Degeneration**
Openness, concern and improved relationships of Stage C PLUS Effective working methods of Stage D	Informality and respect Success emulated by others Happy and rewarding Outside help welcomed Open relationships with other groups	**Stage E** **Maturity**
Operating methods examined Procedures reviewed Problem solving skills developed Frequent review Clear objectives Search for economy Problems handled creatively Team Pride		**Stage D** **Effectiveness**
Members protect team Not working in unified way Not working in methodical way More dynamic and exciting functioning Dormant people begin to contribute Review of operating methods Performance improvement activities undertaken Willingness to experiment Values and assumptions debated Risky issues opened up Leadership or management discussed Personal animosities dealt with Inward-looking Better listening		**Stage C** **Experimentation**
Team leader performance evaluated Relationships more significant Alliances and cliques formed Personal strengths/weaknesses known Commitment debated Interest in climate Team needs come to the fore Differences expressed more openly		**Stage B** **Infighting**
Testing out Feelings kept hidden Conforming to established line Apprehensive of change Authority central Little listening Little care for others Personal weaknesses covered up Mistakes used as evidence Objectives poorly set Objectives poorly communicated		**Stage A** **Ritual sniffing**

Table 4.1 Stages of Team Development – Summary Chart

Key Teams with a Threshold Requirement	Team Index %	Stage of Team Development (A to F)	Priority for Teambuilding (allocate points out of 10)

Fig. 4.3 Teambuilding Priorities Worksheet

Part III: Is the team ready for teambuilding?

5 Teambuilding Readiness

In the last chapter we identified which teams require teambuilding. Not all teams which need this intervention are ready. In this chapter we identify the components of teambuilding readiness.

Readiness is important because teambuilding deals with real issues and is a confronting intervention. An example makes the point. Recently the authors were asked to act as consultants to a team running a large factory in Holland. An early meeting with the team manager revealed that he felt concerned about the proposed teambuilding intervention and contemplated not attending. Further data collection revealed that team members harboured a great deal of hostility as they felt that the team manager had failed to protect their team's interests in senior management circles. Following a data feedback session the team manager decided to attend a personal development programme and receive personal coaching. A year later this manager felt stronger and held the teambuilding session – which achieved all its objectives. In our opinion an earlier teambuilding intervention would have brought to the surface issues that the team manager could not have coped with whilst the team members lacked the skills to give support, resulting in a destructive experience.

Team building has a high probability of being successful if the following preconditions are met:

1. Team members are willing to open themselves to the process.
2. The team can cope with the challenges of teambuilding.
3. The organisation is supportive of teambuilding efforts.

An instrument, the Teambuilding Readiness Survey, is included in the next chapter. It will help you to assess whether a particular team is suitable for a teambuilding approach. In the final analysis this is a question of judgement but the Teambuilding Readiness Survey helps to structure the decision making process.

One important question should be asked at this stage – 'Who should take the decision about whether a team is ready?' Ideally the answer is 'The client'. However, one of the primary causes of unreadiness is the team manager's lack of willingness or skills. Accordingly, the teambuilding facilitator, in the opinion of the authors, should have the final say. If a key team is judged to be 'unready' then other interventions – principally training, coaching and counselling – should be applied.

The Teambuilding Readiness Survey has 12 items. Each has a bearing on the readiness of the team (some factors are weighted more highly than others). We will now examine each item to explain its connection with the concept of teambuilding readiness.

READINESS AREAS

1 IS THE TEAM WILLING TO COMMIT THE NECESSARY TIME?

A teambuilding intervention is a crucial change to the sub-culture and working practices of a group. It requires extensive diagnosis and time to explore all of the relevant issues. A superficial examination of a team's functioning often leads to frustration and little change. If a team is not prepared to spend time 'contemplating its own navel' then a teambuilding intervention is likely to fail. In practice, significant progress can be made within a three day period, but many teambuilding programmes require a sequence of interventions (normally off site workshops) over months. The decision to invest time is an important test of the team's commitment.

2 ARE THE FUNDS MADE AVAILABLE?

Willingness to spend money is usually, but not always, a second test of commitment. The amount of money is a poor indicator since a sum considered excessive by a children's home staff team could be a flea bite to a multi-national corporation. In practice, much can be achieved on a low budget but the willingness to spend development funds is a good indicator of willingness to take teambuilding seriously.

Funds are necessary for off site expenses (hotels and so on) and retaining the services of a facilitator. Some organisations may have an internal facilitating resource but often an external consultant is required. However, the per-head cost is often low as consultants' fees are charged on a daily basis.

3 DOES THE TEAM MANAGER WANT TO UNDERTAKE TEAMBUILDING?

The team manager's willingness to participate fully is a critical factor. Sometimes teams are selected for teambuilding by someone other than the client group (perhaps as a 'last ditch' attempt by a senior manager to sort out a problem). However, since the team manager will receive confronting feedback and must coach the team to improve, it is essential that he or she is a willing participant.

The authors' experience leads them to conclude that considerable enthusiasm is more than can be expected (especially for a 'first timer') but a basic willingness to be exposed, open, and supportive is required. In effect, the team manager must be prepared to be 'the client'. Occasionally managers agree to go ahead with team building but later they get 'cold feet' and withdraw, leaving the team in more disarray than before. Whenever possible, this should be avoided.

Another important point to note is that team members look to their leader for signs (often subtle) as to his/her commitment. Without ownership of the intervention by the manager little of value can be achieved.

4 DO THE TEAM MEMBERS WANT TO UNDERTAKE TEAMBUILDING?

All team members must be willing to open themselves to the process. This does not mean that they are unreservedly positive: that is too much to ask. Rather that all participants should have given their informed consent for the intervention to proceed. Reservations and uncertainties are to be expected. Without a basic willingness from team members the intervention is likely to be soured by game playing, cynicism and lack of disclosure. Sometimes a strong team member can sabotage a whole intervention. Often reservation or opposition is rooted in fear and such anxieties can be diminished by a full explanation of the methodologies to be used.

Enthusiastic and wholehearted support by all team members for the teambuilding process is a strong positive indicator and increases the probability that successful outcomes will follow.

5 ARE TEAM MEMBERS TRAINED IN INTERPERSONAL SKILLS?

Over the past twenty years we have seen a vast development in interpersonal skills training. Many topics have been covered so that an array of behavioural skills can be developed which include:

- assertion
- listening
- communication
- joint problem solving
- leadership behaviours
- motivating
- action planning

Much interpersonal skills training is based on values of collaboration, openness, authenticity and evaluating difference – all values which are central to the teambuilding process.

If some (ideally all) members of the team have been through such interpersonal skills training the probability of success is enhanced because there is less

51

likelihood of a values clash and team members are more able to contribute actively and positively.

Of particular value is training in communication as without the ability to exchange views, data, feelings and ideas it is difficult to resolve team issues.

6 IS THE TEAM MANAGER RESPECTED?

We have made the point earlier that the team manager's role is central in many teambuilding interventions. Sometimes the team manager is not well respected. The teambuilding process will bring this issue to the surface which will place the team manager under enormous pressure in a public forum which can lead either to a dramatic breakthrough or a profound sense of failure.

Team managers almost always receive negative feedback during teambuilding events but when this becomes the dominant theme the teambuilding intervention is a high risk intervention for the client group. This is not to say that a teambuilding intervention is always hazardous when the team manager is not respected. However, progress can only be made in such a situation if the team manager is willing and able to face the team's negative views and adopt new behaviour subsequently.

7 DOES THE TEAM HAVE A SUBSTANTIAL SHARED TASK?

As we discussed earlier in this book, only groups with a need to work together can be developed as teams. Accordingly, teams respond best to teambuilding if there is a real and significant need for them to work together in a co-operative and interdependent manner. Only if the team has a need to be effective will the members be seriously committed to teambuilding.

There are six dimensions of interdependence, outlined in the table below:

1	**Interdependent Tasks** (team members must work directly together)
2	**Co-operation for Mutually Dependent Tasks** (team members must co-operate)
3	**Clarification of Domains and Roles** (team members must clarify areas of responsibility)
4	**Learning and Performance Enhancement** (team members learn from each other)
5	**Uniform Policies and Procedures** (team members adhere to common standards)
6	**Shared Values** (team members share basic philosophies and principles)

Table 5.1 Levels of Team Interdependence

Teams may require teambuilding to enhance performance at one or more of these levels (often all six are relevant). If there is no requirement for team work at any of these levels it is right to ask the question 'Why bother to develop the team at all?'

8   HAVE MEMBERS OF THE TEAM EXPERIENCED A POSITIVE TEAMBUILDING EVENT BEFORE?

The benefits of teambuilding are intellectually appealing but become even more persuasive when experienced for real. To the uninitiated the teambuilding process can appear mysterious, frightening or obscure. Such emotional reactions are lessened if one or more members of the team have been through a similar (successful!) experience on a previous occasion. Prior exposure helps people realise the potential of teambuilding and they can support others as they go through the process.

It is important to note that previous exposure to a negative teambuilding event can have exactly the opposite impact. Scepticism, perhaps even fear, is increased. Much work will then need to be done to explore the causes of anxiety and build credibility for the process about to be undertaken. Often the stature and values of the facilitator are key factors.

9   DOES THE TEAM HAVE ACCESS TO A COMPETENT FACILITATOR?

Teams often benefit from the help of a facilitator – who may be internal to the organisation or an external resource. Like any management technique the team approach needs to be learned. Team building is a well defined process which is difficult to 'just pick up'. Often a guide is necessary.

A competent facilitator acts as a catalyst, process consultant, observer, coach, data collector, action planner and empowerer during the teambuilding process. He or she needs specialised training and a breadth of experience. Teambuilding facilitators may come from within the organisation (and have the advantage that they are familiar) or outside (and have the advantage that they are more objective).

Facilitators need a depth of experience (we explore the skill requirements later in this book). From time to time teams 'sail into troubled waters'. It is here that expert help is an invaluable source of strength. It is wrong to leave a team 'stuck in the mire' if expert facilitators can achieve a breakthrough. Facilitators provide the team with a 'security blanket'!

External facilitators bring the additional benefit that they can offer comparative data and experience and are more likely to confront issues head on (since their main job is not threatened). They may also have more inherent credibility than an internal resource and so be able to work with senior clients more easily.

10 DOES THE TEAM MEET?

This seems like an obvious point but it is more important than it first appears. In order for a team to develop, all the members must collect together for team meetings fairly often. Unless this happens the team lacks a collective life and teambuilding progress will not be sustained.

Interestingly, it is not always necessary for team members to meet in person. The development of video conferencing in the 1990s permitted the application of team building techniques to groups which worked together but were physically separated – perhaps by thousands of miles.

The development of informal relationships is a highly desirable adjunct to formal teamworking. In the last analysis it is desirable for team members to like each other! Otherwise the quality of caring and support is lacking, causing a degradation of the key team ethic of support and openness.

11 IS THERE SENIOR MANAGEMENT SUPPORT FOR TEAMBUILDING?

Team managers are influenced by their bosses. If a manager is told 'In this organisation we work as a team and I want to agree your objectives for team development', that is a powerful force promoting teambuilding.

Organisations where the team approach is understood and supported by top managers have a much more favourable climate for teambuilding. Without such support useful work can still be done as most teams enjoy some autonomy. However, organisational support makes things easier.

12 IS THE TEAM'S FUNCTIONING CRITICAL TO ORGANISATIONAL PERFORMANCE?

The topic of team effectiveness has been dealt with in the previous chapter but it recurs here because of the impact of perceived importance of effective teamwork on the psyche of the group. Teams that perceive their role to be crucial are more disposed to invest energy and commitment into team development because they sense the centrality of their contribution. Conversely a team that perceives itself to be insignificant is less likely to be disposed towards an organisationally-orientated team approach; here there is the possibility that teambuilding could increase a feeling of disaffection and disenchantment.

6 The Teambuilding Readiness Survey

PURPOSE

Team development efforts are more likely to be beneficial if the team is ready to undertake a teambuilding process. The Teambuilding Readiness Survey will help you evaluate whether a particular team is a good 'candidate' for an intervention.

METHOD

Complete the instrument by circling a number for each item.

THE SURVEY

Clearly define the team being assessed.

> The team being assessed is ....

1 How much time is the team willing to dedicate to teambuilding?

None	1–2 Days	3–4 Days	5 Days or more
-3	2	3	4

2 How much money is the team willing to dedicate to teambuilding?

None	Less than 5% of the Team's Manpower Development Budget (MDB)	6–10% of MDB	11%+ of MDB
-3	2	3	4

3 Does the team manager *want* to lead the teambuilding process?

No	Somewhat	Eager
-6	2	6

4 Do team members *want* to participate in a teambuilding process?

No	Somewhat	Eager
0	2	4

5 Have team members experienced a training programme in interpersonal skills?

None	1–2 Members	3 or more
0	1	2

6 How much is the team manager respected by the team?

No Respect	Conditional Respect	Full Respect
-5	3	5

7 Does the team have significant shared tasks?

No Shared Tasks	Significant Shared Tasks	Crucial Shared Tasks
-4	2	4

8 Does anyone in the team have previous experience of teambuilding?

Negative Previous Experience	No Previous Experience	Positive Previous Experience
-2	0	2

9 Is there an experienced facilitator available to the team?

No	Yes	Outstandingly Competent
0	2	4

10 Does the team meet together?

No	Sometimes	Often	Very Often
-5	2	4	6

11 Do top management support teambuilding?

No	Lukewarm	Positive	Very Positive
-2	0	2	4

12 How important is the team's task to the organisation as a whole?

Unimportant	Some Significance	Very Significant
-3	3	6

SCORING

Add your scores for each of the twelve items and note the total below.

Total $\boxed{}$

If the score is less than 20:
The team is probably not well prepared. Other development strategies (training, coaching, counselling, team meetings and so on) will help to increase readiness.

If the score is 21 – 40:
The team may be ready for teambuilding but careful contracting is required to try to increase the readiness scores in as many dimensions as possible. A lower risk teambuilding intervention may be appropriate which creates the preconditions of openness and positive climate.

If the score is 41 or more:
Go for it!

Part IV: Does the organisation have competent teambuilding resources?

7 The Competences of Team Development Facilitators

Some teams are both able and willing to develop themselves. Many effective team leaders shape their team's growth by their day-by-day management style and occasional off site workshops. Perhaps the team leader uses team theory and standardised exercises to structure teambuilding events. However, many teams are unable, for one reason or another, to manage their own team development process and for these teams the only choice is to invite a facilitator to work with them.

The key options are summarised in the table below:

	Team Status	Facilitation Style
1	Team has members experienced in teambuilding and is willing to develop	Can self-facilitate
2	Experienced team beginning to become complacent	Confronting facilitation beneficial
3	Maturing team learning to be effective	Teamwork skills coach helpful
4	New/developing team working through basic issues but lacking experience	Team building facilitator important
5	Fractured or conflicted team	Therapeutic facilitation very valuable

Table 7.1   Key Options in the Team Development Process

The role of the facilitator is complex. The seven key dimensions of the role are:

1. Data Collection: providing mechanisms for the collection of objective and meaningful data about the climate, leadership, functions, processes and effectiveness of the team within the context of its suppliers and customers.
2. Workshop Design: developing programmes for teambuilding which address team blockages and facilitate a transformation of team climate, leadership, functions, processes and effectiveness.

3. Coaching: providing guidance to the team leader and team members in increasing their effectiveness. This includes skill development and review of personal performance.
4. Confronting: encouraging the team to review the impact of behaviour – both on each other and on performance. Significant, but non-expressed, issues are brought to the surface and explored.
5. Energising: conveying a sense of optimism and the possibility of a better future. Often energising support needs to be given when difficult issues need to be resolved.
6. Conceptualising: providing ways to understand complex issues. This may include the explication of theories, models and conceptual frameworks.
7. Action Planning: transforming insights about what needs to be done into realisable action plans. Objective setting, success criteria specification, delegation and planning are key requirements.

The facilitator's role varies according to the needs of the team. However, interventions based on behavioural science use a 14 step common methodology which is summarised in the chart below:

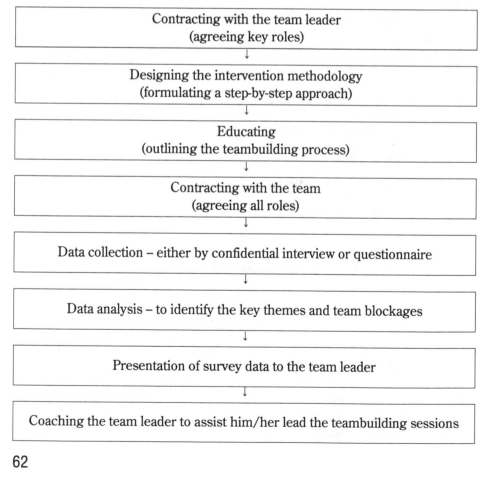

| Contracting with the team leader |
| (agreeing key roles) |

↓

| Designing the intervention methodology |
| (formulating a step-by-step approach) |

↓

| Educating |
| (outlining the teambuilding process) |

↓

| Contracting with the team |
| (agreeing all roles) |

↓

| Data collection – either by confidential interview or questionnaire |

↓

| Data analysis – to identify the key themes and team blockages |

↓

| Presentation of survey data to the team leader |

↓

| Coaching the team leader to assist him/her lead the teambuilding sessions |

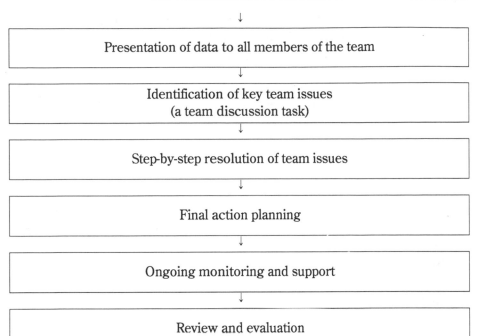

Facilitating a team through this 14 step process clearly requires a battery of consulting skills, the most significant of which are:

1. Contracting: forming agreements which clarify roles and mutual responsibilities.
2. Data gathering: collecting objective and comprehensive data on team effectiveness issues.
3. Data analysis: grouping ideas and defining key issues. Understanding cause and effect chains.
4. Giving feedback: presenting data comprehensively and assisting groups to come to terms with unexpected or confronting issues.
5. Coaching: helping team members make the best use of data and developing both mind-sets and skills needed to overcome blockages.
6. Structured problem-solving and decision making: assisting groups to work through complex issues using a variety of problem solving and decision making tools.
7. Action planning: transforming insights into plans. Recording what needs to be done and who will do it by what dates.
8. Supporting: giving encouragement and empowerment to assist the team to overcome difficulties and work together openly, fully and effectively.

Such consulting skills come from different sources. Clearly team facilitators generally not only need to be experts in interpersonal skills but they also require specific expertise in problem solving and decision making.

From this analysis of the seven areas of conceptual and behavioural skills we can define the underlying attributes which lead to superior performance as a team facilitator. These we define as team facilitation competences.

TEAM FACILITATION COMPETENCES

1   STRONG THEORY BASE

Effective team facilitators know a great deal about their subject. They have read and discussed widely and deeply. There is a growing body of technical literature (some of it supported by research data) on team development. Often helpful presentations are made at specialist conferences. This should be understood and conceptualised into models which can be used to structure interventions.

2   MODEL OF TEAM GROWTH

The facilitator needs to have a deep understanding of the stages of team development. This is important for two reasons: firstly, the intervention focus and style of the team facilitator changes according to the current stage of development of the team; secondly, teams often benefit from having brief inputs (or 'lecturettes') on stages of team growth so that they can position themselves on a development path. It is especially helpful if teams clearly realise what has to be done to make progress.

3   EXTENSIVE REPERTOIRE OF 'LECTURETTES'

There are few teambuilding sessions when it is not necessary for the facilitator to present ideas, concepts, models or frameworks. These enable team members to conceptualise their current situation in order to provide a language for working through outstanding issues. Many issues may need to be covered including: behavioural and interpersonal skills, leadership, team roles, team climate, problem solving methodology, control, creativity, co-ordination, inter-team relations and so on. Experienced facilitators develop hundreds of such 'lecturettes' and find that they are often called upon to present without preparation, just because the time is right.

4   AVAILABILITY OF STRUCTURED EXPERIENCES AND INSTRUMENTS

This point is similar to item three above except that the facilitator requires a repertoire of structured activities and instruments which may be the best way of focusing the team's development energy on blockages and development opportunities. Such materials are the 'software' of training and can be an important dimension in team development. Not only does the facilitator need to have a library of such materials, but he or she also needs to understand the administration process and its likely impact.

5   DATA COLLECTION AND PROCESSING SKILLS

Often team development requires the collection of valid data and its subsequent organisation into meaningful categories. There are several skills relevant to this task (which is an information processing based activity). For example, facilitators need to be able to: gain empathy and rapport with team members, design survey questionnaires and interview schedules, probe sensitive issues, record data objectively, cluster ideas into categories, perform basic statistical tests and clarify issues without imposing judgement.

6   PRESENTING DATA AND GIVING FEEDBACK

There is an art to presentation of survey data. Complex information, especially if it is confronting or emotionally charged, requires careful communication. It can overwhelm or confuse if presented badly. The facilitator needs to reveal data at a pace determined by the group. All significant data has to be presented otherwise the facilitator is lacking in openness and denies the team its own truth.

There is a second aspect to this competence. Often the facilitator will need to confront the team and individuals with his/her views of the impact of their behaviour. This includes a capacity to give 'real time' feedback and is especially useful in conflicted or 'stuck' groups.

7   COACHING

The fundamental skills required by a facilitator are 'coaching' which we define as 'helping the group to adopt behaviours likely to result in enhanced performance'. Coaching skills are often required as they assist the team (and separately the team leader) to rehearse better ways of resolving issues and achieving potential. The skill set includes performance evaluation learning.

8   PERSONAL ACCEPTABILITY

This competence area is difficult to define as, in the end, it boils down to saying that 'the team must trust the facilitator'. Trust requires such attributes as: integrity, empathy-building, authenticity, stature and rounded competences. There is no doubt that the facilitator has to win a special place in the hearts and minds of team members. Like a therapist, the team becomes dependent on the facilitator to some extent as it undertakes a process of teambuilding. The personal qualities of the facilitator need to be such that he/she is perceived as a 'good guide'.

9 CO-FACILITATING EXPERTISE

Sometimes team facilitators will work with others (in effect, forming a team themselves). Here the team effectiveness attributes which the facilitators are seeking to engender in others need to be practised! Competence is enhanced by working with other professionals and seeing how they approach facilitation challenges. Facilitation is a 'craft'. As the medieval craftsmen discovered, it is necessary to have a long apprenticeship before mastery is gained.

10 AUTHENTICITY AND OPENNESS

We believe that the team facilitator needs to be 'true to his/her feelings and values'. Many of the most important insights which guide interventions are felt rather than thought. The wisdom of the emotions is sometimes more powerful than the virtues of rationality and analysis. Such intuitive or sensing skills virtually become 'second nature' and the development of an 'informed intuition' is a major task for team facilitators. This only happens when the facilitator listens to him/herself and is true to his or her feelings.

THE TEAMBUILDER'S CODE

These ten facilitator's competences need to be developed into behaviourally specific guidelines in order to be useful. We find the Teambuilder's Code a useful way to encapsulate the messages.

A Teambuilder strives to respect individual differences within effective teams. The teambuilder strives to:

1. Gain organisational acceptance by:
   - ensuring that teambuilding aims and techniques are widely understood
   - building support for teambuilding initiatives
   - acquiring resources for teambuilding

2. Be objective by:
   - collecting valid data
   - being comprehensive
   - not judging or evaluating

3. Be flexible by:
   - adapting to individuals
   - following the team's objectives
   - avoiding excessive structure

4. Work step-by-step by:
   - starting modestly, letting success build confidence
   - recognising that people are more comfortable with things they can grasp themselves
   - not overwhelming team members with data

5. Agree 'contracts' by:
   - being clear about roles
   - knowing what he or she will not do
   - sticking to agreements
   - getting commitment early

6. Respect the client by:
   - recognising that development is basically self regulating
   - accepting that people cannot be forced into attitude change
   - knowing that feelings are as important as thoughts
   - challenging the client's judgements but accepting that ultimately the client's decisions must prevail

7. Ensure that interventions are relevant by:
   - relating interventions to everyday life
   - ensuring insight is balanced with action
   - planning specific changes
   - providing mechanisms for on-going development

8. Reduce the risk of negative outcomes by:
   - protecting individuals from being brainwashed or manipulated
   - encouraging realism rather than false optimism
   - building a supportive team climate
   - avoiding other teams being disadvantaged

9. Create a positive climate by:
   - developing knowledge and affection between team members
   - giving confidence and encouragement
   - helping the team to meet the needs of individual team members
   - nurturing the team when stress occurs
   - encouraging active listening

10. Look after him/herself by:
    - not discounting one's own needs
    - continuing to learn and develop
    - seeking feedback
    - being authentic

8 The Teambuilder's Competence Audit

PURPOSE

This audit provides a structured format to assess a team facilitator's skills and approach.

INSTRUCTIONS

Work through the audit, putting a mark on each scale to indicate your current position. Answer all of the questions. If possible, check your self-perception with peers and clients in order to provide as objective an assessment as possible. Then complete the scoring section at the end of the chapter.

THE TEAMBUILDER'S AUDIT

1 Background reading

| I have no knowledge of the literature on teambuilding. | 1 2 3 4 5 6 7 | I have read extensively (five books or more) about teambuilding. |

2 Organisational acceptance

| I have not taken steps to gain organisational acceptance for team-building. | 1 2 3 4 5 6 7 | I have ensured that team-building is widely understood and valued by senior managers. |

3 Theory of team growth

I do not have a model of the stages of team growth.	1 2 3 4 5 6 7 I have compared several models of team growth.

4 Flexible approach

I always seek to adhere to pre-determined time tables and schedules.	1 2 3 4 5 6 7 I am willing and able to respond to the needs of the moment.

5 Behavioural science methodology

I believe in feeling and hunch rather than data.	1 2 3 4 5 6 7 I believe in hard data rather than feelings and hunches.

6 Informed consent

I do not seek consent before undertaking an intervention.	1 2 3 4 5 6 7 I take great care to obtain comment from team members for the process to be followed before an intervention is undertaken.

7 Designing events

I lack skills in designing workshops which are balanced and constructive.	1 2 3 4 5 6 7 I have considerable skills in designing workshops which are balanced and constructive.

8 Problem solving and decision making

I am not skilled in the stages of problem solving and decision making methodologies.	1 2 3 4 5 6 7 I am highly skilled in problem solving and decision making methodologies

9 Repertoire of lecturettes and structured activities

I have a very small range of lecturettes and structured experiences.	1 2 3 4 5 6 7 I have a vast range of lecturettes and structured experiences.

10 Giving feedback

I lack skills in presenting data to individuals and teams.	1 2 3 4 5 6 7	I have a depth of skill in presenting data to individuals and teams.

11 Observational skills

I am unpractised in the observation of work groups.	1 2 3 4 5 6 7	I am skilled in the multi-dimensional analysis of work groups.

12 Goal clarification

I do not seek to clarify goals with clients.	1 2 3 4 5 6 7	I always agree a comprehensive goal statement with clients.

13 Realism

I undertake assignments without really considering whether I have the resources to cope.	1 2 3 4 5 6 7	My work is always sufficiently well resourced to be effective.

14 Team linkage

I consider the team as an isolated entity.	1 2 3 4 5 6 7	I ensure that teams review their linkages with other teams in order to build sound inter-team relations.

15 Co-facilitating experience

I have never worked alongside an experienced teambuilder.	1 2 3 4 5 6 7	I have worked with several experienced teambuilders.

16 Personal openness

I often fail to confront difficult or important issues.	1 2 3 4 5 6 7	I always confront difficult or important issues.

17 Energising style

| I fail to rouse people's energy and enthusiasm. | 1 2 3 4 5 6 7 | Almost always I succeed in rousing people's energy and enthusiasm. |

18 Applying learning

| I do not use teambuilding techniques in my own working life. | 1 2 3 4 5 6 7 | I frequently use team-building techniques in my own working life. |

19 Obtaining feedback

| I do not seek feedback on my own behaviour. | 1 2 3 4 5 6 7 | I frequently seek feedback on my own behaviour. |

20 Action planning

| I do not insist that insights become action plans. | 1 2 3 4 5 6 7 | I insist that insights become action plans. |

SCORING THE TEAMBUILDER'S AUDIT

Add your scores for each of the 20 items in the audit. Although the scores are subjective they provide a useful basis for reflection.

Scores		
	20–40	Considerable training needed before teambuilding undertaken
	41–80	Some skills developed but further training needed
	81–100	Quite experienced and well prepared
	100 +	You are an experienced and capable teambuilder

IMPROVING TEAMBUILDING SKILLS

Look at each of the 20 items in the Audit and highlight those where you scored five points or less. Take the lowest scoring items and complete the table below. Repeat for all other highlighted items. (Photocopy table as necessary).

Item Number	Topic	Reasons Why Important	Ideas for Improvement	Action Plan

Table 8.1 Teambuilder's Audit Summary

Part V: Do we need a teambuilding consultant?

9 The Teambuilding Consultant

Although we believe in do-it-yourself approaches to teambuilding wherever possible, there are some circumstances in which teams do benefit from external help in working on their own development. This chapter is about these issues concerning choosing and working with a consultant:

1. When to use a consultant.
2. What kind of consultants can contribute.
3. The competences of an effective consultant.
4. Where to find consultants.
5. How to choose a suitable consultant.
6. The stages of working with a consultant.

WHEN TO USE A CONSULTANT

A consultant can help teams at several stages of their development. For example, in a newly formed team there is a natural apprehension of the team's leaders and members in setting out on an uncharted course. Team leaders may feel particularly exposed, especially if they suspect that 'nasties' may lurk beneath the surface. Some team members may also feel apprehensive about exposing themselves to a new and unknown process.

As their skills develop, teams usually become adept at recognising their own process problems. At first team members may be too engrossed in their individual work to be able to stand back and see what is going on; they can use the perspective of an external agent to help them. While a team is developing, problems and issues may arise that are particularly difficult or sensitive; these call for the skills of a consultant.

As a team matures, it normally develops the ability to handle its own problems and the need for external help either diminishes or disappears. Later, mature and effective teams may want to spend time with a trusted consultant once or twice a year, just to get another perspective on how things are going. This is especially important if the team is to avoid slipping into the degeneration stage discussed earlier in this book.

A consultant is valuable:

- to help start a team development process
- when team leaders and members do not have the skills to manage team development activities
- when there are especially difficult or sensitive issues to be worked through
- when team members feel that they are too involved in task performance to be able to stand back and see what is going on
- to give impartial feedback on team performance and problems
- to prevent a team suffering from 'groupthink' and entering the degeneration stage
- to help a team review its progress from time to time
- when inter-group problems arise which are difficult for the team to handle alone

WHAT CONSULTANTS CAN CONTRIBUTE

A consultant cannot make a team effective; teams do that for themselves. There also is no way in which a consultant can do the work of the team. But a consultant can assist a group in several ways.

Many consultants are 'experts'. Sometimes an organisation simply needs someone who possesses specialist knowledge not contained in the organisation. Once the knowledge is transferred, there is no need for the consultant, who is then paid and leaves. At other times, there are consultants who possess skills that are beyond the capacity of anybody in the organisation. A good example of this is the expert firefighters who put out oil rig fires.

Team development consultancy is different from the two other kinds just mentioned. It is not the *content* of the team's work that is the focus for consultation but the *process* by which members of the team work together. This distinction between *content* and *process* is vital.

A team development consultant is concerned with helping the team to:

- generate valid data about the team's effectiveness
- identify blockages to effective working
- diagnose what is going on inside the team and why blockages exist
- recognise, confront and assist the team to work through the problems themselves
- develop a 'transformational' vision of how it should develop
- set team development objectives, and chart their own progress
- facilitate the development of a mature, open team climate

The consultant's principal contributions are likely to be:

- collecting data about team effectiveness
- observing what is happening between team members as the team works
- serving as a mirror to the team, so that the members have a clear view of their behaviour
- selecting activities that help the team improve its performance
- giving feedback to the team and its members on how they are doing

A team development consultant will not:

- usurp leadership, but will support the manager and each member
- tell the team what is wrong with it (but will help the team to recognise its own difficulties)
- make decisions for the team (but will help the team to make its own decisions)
- get engrossed and involved in the content of the team's work (but will retain objectivity)
- make the team dependent on his or her continued presence (but will work to make the team independent of external help).

Effective team development consultants can provide skills in working sensitivity with groups of people in a helping and supportive way and also offer their comparative experience in working with the problems of many teams. It is these skills and experiences that the team is contracting to obtain.

QUALITIES AND CHARACTERISTICS OF A GOOD TEAM DEVELOPMENT CONSULTANT

We know a brilliant consultant who failed high school, worked as a carpenter for fifteen years, and then by accident became involved in team development work. Another successful consultant started work as an engineer and, through his church membership, became involved in social work and then team development. Another colleague has a degree in psychology and a PhD based on psychotherapy research. One of the worst failures we have encountered in consultancy has a degree in sociology and long experience in social work, clinical psychology, and sociological research. Our conclusion is that a string of academic qualifications is no guarantee that a consultant is effective.

Identifying the characteristics of effective consultants is difficult because of the wide diversity of backgrounds and experience shared by those we have known, but here is our best attempt.

AN EFFECTIVE CONSULTANT

1. He or she is a person who has self knowledge, gained from a breadth and depth of personal experience. This knowledge cannot be developed from text books or academic education. It comes, rather, from working extensively with other people and working through their own personal values. A consultant is likely to manifest these characteristics through behaviours such as:

   - listening actively
   - valuing others as people
   - taking people as they are
   - having space and time for working with others
   - abstaining from personal crusading and dogmatic views
   - clarifying his/her personal values
   - confronting people and issues positively
   - reflecting problems to people in a helpful way

2. He or she has a foundation of practical theory. This does not simply mean an ability to regurgitate other people's theories, impressive though this may seem. It does mean that the individual is able to draw on research and theory in a relevant way to guide his or her work.
3. He or she is open and realistic. Some consultants will promise the world. Others are subtle manipulators who attempt to 'con' or even threaten others into changed behaviours. An effective consultant will be open in giving feedback to others and will be quite explicit about his or her own values. Importantly, he or she will also develop a clear 'contract' at the beginning of an assignment which will define the expectations and responsibilities of both client and consultant.
4. He or she can not only work with the team on the here and now issues, but also encourage the members to visualise ways of improving for the future. However, beware the consultant who lives idealistically always in the future, especially where results are concerned.

WHERE TO FIND CONSULTANTS

When an organisation has no need for a consultant, it may be assailed by publicity material promising dramatic consulting results in every field conceivable – from accounting to Zen meditation.

When there is a specific need, then finding the right consultant may become a challenge. Sometimes it seems as though all the good consultants have migrated to greener fields, are booked for the next year, or were last heard of heading for the desert to write a book.

However, the right consultant can be found somewhere – in business schools, other centres of management education, large and small consultancy firms, inside other companies, and in independent practice. Consultants work under many different titles with the commonest being: group facilitator, group training specialist, change agent, and team developer.

The very best way to find the right *individual* to meet your needs is by personal recommendation from people who have had good experiences. To do this, first check with companies or other organisations who have done some work in team development.

A second approach is asking a local business school to recommend someone. If this fails to produce results, find a management publication containing material relevant to your interests. Then contact the publisher or the author to see if they know of any suitable people. If you still have no success, try the larger consultant firms that specialise in personal skills and group training, or contact the associations of consultants and management associations that exist in most countries.

A word of warning: when approaching large institutions or consultancies, remember that you are going to work with an individual person, not the institution, so check on the person who will be doing the work.

HOW TO CHOOSE A SUITABLE CONSULTANT

It is wise, first, to assess the work of a prospective consultant and look for relevance to your needs and standards of quality. Any consultant worth his salt will be pleased to refer you to past clients; if necessary, phone or visit them.

A second tactic is talking with several consultants and choosing one of them. Discuss your problems with each consultant and work through whatever strategy is proposed. Does it feel right? Realistic? Not too slick? Does the consultant have the 'presence' to make the intervention work? Does he/she listen? Is his/her recommended process 'client centred'?

In working through these issues with you, the consultants should be showing some of the behavioural skills that will be manifest in their work. Reject a consultant such as one who totally disrupted a whole office by his aggressive and pompous telephone behaviour. When this man finally reached the manager and announced that he was a 'specialist in human relations', the manager, having heard the effects of his behaviour, just said, 'I don't believe you!' and hung up.

Another criterion is whether you feel any personal warmth, trust and understanding developing. This is critical because a team development consultant will be working intimately with the team and each one of its members. The initial exploration of problems with a team manager and the team (done before any commitment to work is made) should be deep enough to enable the team to develop a sense of whether it would feel good about working with the consultant.

Something to check as part of the initial 'contract' with a consultant is whether he will devote sufficient time and energy to service your needs.

Finally, can you afford a consultant? Consultancy is not cheap, but an effective consultant can make all the difference to the success of a team's development.

THE STAGES OF WORKING WITH A CONSULTANT

Effective management of the introduction of a consultant to your team or organisation will reduce the risks of a bad experience. The process should include the following steps:

1. Review and identify the group's needs. What issues and problems does the team feel it has? Can these be handled internally or should they be dealt with by somebody in the wider organisation? (Here the Team-Review Questionnaire from Francis and Young, *Improving Work Groups*[1] can be of great use.)
2. Obtain consensus from the team concerning the need for an external consultant. If there is a general feeling that skilled outside help is necessary, then move to the next step.
3. Contact a number of suitable consultants and have them meet other team members.
4. Select the most appropriate consultant following the guidelines suggested earlier.
5. Develop a 'contract with the consultant. This is not so much a formal written document as a mutual understanding that covers such aspects as:

   - the initial diagnosis of the problems to be worked on
   - the method of working on these problems
   - how much further diagnosis is required, and how this will be done
   - the relationship between the consultant and team members (especially the team manager)
   - what roles the consultant normally plays
   - the design of initial activities
   - how progress will be reviewed
   - how success will be judged
   - when work will start
   - the time scale over which work will be carried out
   - the broad amount of consultancy time required
   - how much this will cost and how the consultant will be paid

6. Complete the initial diagnostic work and plan the initial activities. As much as possible, this should be done with and accepted by the whole team. `
7. Start work.

8. Identify how and broadly when the consultant will begin to withdraw from the team. An effective consultant's prime aim will be to bring the team to a position in which it is strong enough to handle its own development without external help. Make sure this issue is raised with the consultant.

At some stage in a team's growth, an outsider may be an essential agent to help unblock problems. But, in the end, the health and effectiveness of any team must be assessed by the team itself.

NOTES

[1] Francis, D. and Young, D. *Improving Work Groups*, University Associates, San Diego, 1989

10 The Team Development Consultant Audit

PURPOSE

Managers and trainers can be bombarded by would-be advisers and consultants. The relationship between company and consultant is always close and sometimes the outcomes are invaluable. The Team Development Consultant Audit will help you get maximum benefit from your investment in consultant help.

Use Part A to consider whether outside help is required in a specific situation.

Part B should be used as a checklist to ensure that essential points are covered in any discussion with a consultant you are considering engaging.

PART A – DO WE NEED AN EXTERNAL CONSULTANT?

INSTRUCTIONS

Go through the checklist and circle a number between one and five in each case to illustrate your assessment of the status of the selected team in relation to the item.

THE ITEMS

1   Is the team's performance critical to the organisation?

The team's performance is not critical	1 2 3 4 5	The team's performance is critical

2   Does the organisation possess a competent internal team facilitator?

No internal team facilitator available	1 2 3 4 5	Highly skilled team facilitator available

85

3 Does the team present unusual or difficult 'problems'?

No unusual or difficult 'problems'	├─┼─┼─┼─┤ 1 2 3 4 5	Unusual or difficult 'problems' present

4 Does the team manager want to use an external resource?

The team manager prefers an internal resource	├─┼─┼─┼─┤ 1 2 3 4 5	The team manager prefers an external resource

5 Is the team very senior?

The team is not senior	├─┼─┼─┼─┤ 1 2 3 4 5	The team is very senior

6 Does the internal team facilitator want to work with an external consultant?

The internal team facilitator wants to work alone	├─┼─┼─┼─┤ 1 2 3 4 5	The internal team facilitator wants to work with an external consultant

7 Can internal team facilitators meet the team manager's time scales?

Time scales can be met by internal team facilitators	├─┼─┼─┼─┤ 1 2 3 4 5	Time scales cannot be met by internal team facilitators

8 Is the internal team facilitator considered too much 'part of the system' to deal with likely issues?

The internal team facilitator is considered to be objective and confidential	├─┼─┼─┼─┤ 1 2 3 4 5	The internal team facilitator is not considered to be objective and confidential

9 Is the target team specialising in an area that is unfamiliar to the internal team facilitator?

The target team's area is familiar to the internal team facilitator	├─┼─┼─┼─┤ 1 2 3 4 5	The target team's area is unfamiliar to the internal team facilitator

10 Does the corporate teambuilding effort need 'fresh blood' and a new approach?

The corporate teambuilding effort is innovative and progressive	1 2 3 4 5	The corporate teambuilding effort is not innovative or progressive

SCORING

Add your scores. These are the implications:

Scores		
	10 – 20	No requirement for an external team consultant
	21 – 30	Possible requirement for an external team consultant
	31 – 40	Probable requirement for an external team consultant
	41 – 50	Definite requirement for an external team consultant

PART B – IS THIS CONSULTANT THE RIGHT ONE FOR US?

INSTRUCTIONS

Interview the prospective consultant and then complete the checklist below. Compare the different consultations using the criteria below. Circle a number between one and five in each case to illustrate your assessment of the consultant in relation to the items.

THE ITEMS

1 Does the consultant have considerable experience of teambuilding?

The consultant is inexperienced	1 2 3 4 5	The consultant has three years' experience or more

2 Does the consultant show interest in your particular needs?

The consultant offers a 'package'	1 2 3 4 5	The consultant is very interested in our particular needs

3 Does the consultant appear to have sufficient 'stature' to command the respect of the target team(s)?

| The consultant lacks 'stature' | ┼─┼─┼─┼─┼
1 2 3 4 5 | The consultant has substantial 'stature' |

4 Does the consultant offer a client centred methodology?

| The methodology is consultant driven | ┼─┼─┼─┼─┼
1 2 3 4 5 | The methodology is client centred |

5 Does the consultant have proven expertise in similar industries?

| The consultant lacks industry expertise | ┼─┼─┼─┼─┼
1 2 3 4 5 | The consultant has great industry expertise |

6 Does the consultant have proven expertise with managers/specialists at similar organisational levels?

| The consultant is inexperienced at the intended organisational level | ┼─┼─┼─┼─┼
1 2 3 4 5 | The consultant is highly experienced at the intended organisational level |

7 Do you feel that the consultant's approach would teach new skills and techniques?

| The consultant's approach has little to teach us | ┼─┼─┼─┼─┼
1 2 3 4 5 | The consultant's approach has much to teach us |

8 Does the consultant have sufficient time and energy to take on the assignment?

| The consultant lacks time or energy | ┼─┼─┼─┼─┼
1 2 3 4 5 | The consultant has time and energy |

9 Is the consultant offering a service which is good value for money?

| The consultant is too expensive | ┼─┼─┼─┼─┼
1 2 3 4 5 | The consultant's fees are 'just right' |

10   Has the consultant developed a rapport with the manager of the target team?

No rapport has been built	$\vdash\!\!+\!\!+\!\!+\!\!\dashv$ 1 2 3 4 5	Considerable rapport has been built

11   Is the consultant willing to disengage when the assignment is complete?

The consultant is seeking to 'capture' the team	$\vdash\!\!+\!\!+\!\!+\!\!\dashv$ 1 2 3 4 5	The consultant is seeking to make the team independent

12   Has the consultant a track record of being innovative and creative?

The consultant has no record of innovation or creativity	$\vdash\!\!+\!\!+\!\!+\!\!\dashv$ 1 2 3 4 5	The consultant has a record of innovation and creativity

13   Are the consultant's values consistent with yours?

The consultant's values are not consistent	$\vdash\!\!+\!\!+\!\!+\!\!\dashv$ 1 2 3 4 5	The consultant's values are totally consistent

14   Does the consultant emphasise the need for 'real-life application' of ideas developed in team building sessions?

The consultant does not emphasise the application of ideas	$\vdash\!\!+\!\!+\!\!+\!\!\dashv$ 1 2 3 4 5	The consultant emphasises the application of ideas

15   Does the consultant have a strong base of theory to support his methodology of teambuilding?

The consultant has a low theory base	$\vdash\!\!+\!\!+\!\!+\!\!\dashv$ 1 2 3 4 5	The consultant has a high theory base

SCORING

Add your scores; these are the implications:

DO WE NEED A TEAMBUILDING CONSULTANT?

Scores	15 – 45	Think again!
	46 – 55	Possible choice
	56 – 65	Probable choice
	66 – 75	Sign now!

Part VI: Building effective teams

11 The Eleven Building Blocks of Effective Teamwork

The atmosphere in the board room was heavy and intense. The senior managers in the organisation had received a shock. One division of the business had been expected to return a handsome profit until a recent audit revealed that basic accounting flaws had led to pricing policies that would result in a substantial loss. The chief executive said, 'I don't want to be unfair but the way I feel at the moment one of you is going to be hung, drawn and quartered for this. When I was at Group Headquarters the company chairman said to me, "You've just used up six of your nine lives." So give it to me straight. Where did we go wrong?'

There was a pause and one manager said, 'Well, the problem is that no one is specifically responsible for relating cost projections to market forecasts. We operate functionally and the only person with an overall view is you as Chief Executive. You are the hub; we all feed information in to you and you are the only one who can make overall decisions.' The other managers nodded in agreement with this analysis of their managerial process but the Chief Executive said, 'You can't expect me to understand all that detail. It's your job to make the decisions work and you must have been aware that something was wrong.' There was a pause before one group member cleared his throat with nervous tension and said, 'I think that several of us are nervous about highlighting problems because experience suggests that we are likely to be up to our ears in manure if we speak up.' The Chief Executive said, 'Well, two things are clear to me: firstly we are organised badly if mistakes like this can occur, and secondly there needs to be much more frankness and openness in our relations with one another. How are we going to improve matters?'

The Chief Executive was asking a vital question which could be re-worded as 'How can we build our team?' Almost every one of us has found ourselves as a member of a team which fails to identify or achieve its objectives. Team relationships are sometimes lifeless, defensive, ineffective, unsatisfying and confusing. This is a costly defect in any organisation since much planning and decision making depends on group effectiveness; managing in a turbulent environment requires that people come together to co-ordinate resources, initiate and progress ideas, gain commitment to common goals and collectively manage complex operations.

managers claim to practise a team approach but fewer have a clear
rstanding of what this means in practice. Only in recent years have we
rly diagnosed the characteristics of effective teams and learned to express
nem in down-to-earth terms. It is now possible to develop the skills which will
enable us to build deliberately an effective team out of an unco-ordinated collection of individuals.

Teambuilding is a conscious process to develop the kind of team which consistently achieves good results. The development of an effective team can be
compared with the growth of a child from infancy to adulthood. There are
many steps to maturity which cannot always be exactly predicted but, as we
saw earlier in the stages of the Team Development Model, there is an overall process through which most teams go on their route to achieving effectiveness.

The team has been rightly described as 'the most powerful tool known to man'
because it has the capacity to generate a uniquely stimulating, supporting and
energetic climate which is enjoyed and valued by individuals and which also
generates achievement of a high order.

However, the team approach is not a panacea for all management problems. It
offers a useful tool for managing groups which have the potential to work
together and accomplish common tasks. The need for direct relationships must
be real. The case for team building is potent. Many working groups are responsible for planning, innovation and sustaining a high level of output but they fail
to use the ability and competence of individual members.

The development of teams from an immature collection of squabbling individuals to a close and effective unit is often fascinating. In essence the process
requires that the group creates a vision of a better future and openly examines
its role and functioning, identifies difficulties and learns, through experiment,
how to overcome its problems. Teambuilding sessions are journeys, as members of the group create an emotional bond between one another. Teambuilding
needs to be undertaken with the intention of enquiry and not as a technique for
pillorying the team manager or any members of the group. In medieval England
vagabonds were locked in wooden restrainers known as stocks. Whilst they
were there, local villagers would throw eggs and rotten fruit at the unfortunate
people transfixed in the stocks. Teambuilding could, in malicious hands, be seen
to have exactly the same function. Teambuilding demands that everyone works
for the benefit of the group rather than scoring points and gaining personal
advantage.

The critical test of team effectiveness is the capacity to achieve useful results.
It is not easy to create a team. Roles have to be balanced, relationships built,
objectives defined, work methods clarified and an energetic and positive climate
created. Effective teams have to be methodically and painstakingly constructed.
It is amazing how frequently managers and team leaders fail to realise that they
have to work hard to fashion an effective team. They can so easily end up with

94

squabbles, gossip circles and secret societies which fail to harness the potential of their membership.

Teambuilding programmes cannot be sustained without the commitment of the team leader who must take an active role, but the exact specification of appropriate leadership behaviour will depend upon the stage of maturity of the group and the quality of external help available. Less developed groups require more sustained assistance than well developed ones.

The team leader should be aware of the needs of the group and have sufficient insight into the concept of teambuilding to help steer the group through the series of developmental stages. An open approach is vital. All issues affecting the group need to be talked through, feedback given and received, and time spent in clarifying expectations. The team leader must demonstrate by his or her own behaviour the high level of openness which is an essential characteristic of the team approach.

The team leader has to be watchful towards team members. Their individual needs have to be identified and each developed as the work of the team continues. In external relations the leader is an advocate and monitors the team boundaries. A close watch needs to be kept on the relationship between the team and the rest of the organisation. The impact of the team's operations on the wider organisation has to be reviewed and areas for investigation, problem solving and building better relationships identified. One useful way to think about a team is to view it as an 'input-output' system with information or material coming in, being processed and emerging as a more valuable, different 'product' at the end. These are internal suppliers and customers. The team leader often influences the inputs and the conditions in which processes occur by access to other parts of the organisation. Accordingly the team leadership role requires additional skills to influence others and to gain adequate resources and support.

Some teams are much more effective than others. This can be seen most clearly on the sports field. It is ironic that a collection of excellent individual players brought together to represent their country may fail to work as a team and their results may then prove a national disgrace. Good teamwork requires more than individual competence.

However, beware: one of the risks of team working is that individual differences can be subsumed into a common viewpoint. This has been called 'groupthink' and is destructive to decision making quality. However, teams can develop processes which mitigate the effects of 'groupthink'[1]. Such actions include:

- setting up sub-groups to explore issues independent of the group
- the team deliberately exploring several options to each decision
- values and assumptions which underly decisions being made explicit
- senior members of the team withholding their views until others have spoken
- all team members being expected to give their views on all major issues

- brief but comprehensive position papers being used to prepare team members to contribute to a discussion
- views of people outside the team being solicited to check thinking
- 'outsiders' being invited into the team to give an independent perspective
- a team norm being developed that challenge is legitimate and rewarded
- extensive use of formal brainstorming and creativity techniques

Some teams develop a team climate which appears to be constructive but is, in fact, destructive. Our term for this is 'conspiracy of niceness' – meaning that team members put etiquette before objectivity. Such teams show the following characteristics, namely:

- negative feelings are unexpressed
- positive feelings are 'manufactured' and expressed excessively
- a 'don't rock the boat' philosophy is adopted
- confronting views are withheld
- risky stances are not adopted
- unpleasant news is played down or kept secret
- there is emphasis on status and position rather than objective achievement
- extreme respect for people, resulting in deference
- a concentration on social events
- rewards are given to amiable people rather than to high performers
- there is major emphasis on 'saving face'

Such teams become complacent and lose their capacity to be an effective organisational building block. Accordingly it is wrong to regard a team as always being constructive. Sometimes there is a clear rationale for a team but the existing team's climate is functionally negative.

The authors have studied hundreds of teams and analysed those which have been particularly successful. From our experience over the last 30 years it is clear to us that successful teams are usually those which have undergone a process of formal or informal teambuilding and which have dealt with eleven key aspects of functioning and performance. If one, or more, of these key aspects is missing or underdeveloped the team will fail to achieve its full potential. We call them the Eleven Building Blocks of Team Effectiveness. They are:

1. Balanced roles.
2. Clear objectives and agreed goals.
3. Openness and confrontation.
4. Support and trust.
5. Co-operation and conflict.
6. Sound procedures.
7. Appropriate leadership.
8. Regular review.
9. Individual development.

10. Sound intergroup relations.
11. Good communications.

Over the following pages we give an outline of these 'building blocks'.

1 BALANCED ROLES

One of the great strengths of the effective team lies in its capacity to use a blend of talents and abilities. Truly effective teams are able to use different personalities to suit a wide range of situations but they can only do this if the mix of team membership is balanced. Too often work teams are formed without any conscious effort to ensure that membership is balanced; but senior managers are increasingly realising that 'balancing' is worth the effort. Good teambuilding begins with good staff selection. Just as the master chef has to choose between ingredients, ensure their quality and determine the correct quantities, so the teambuilder has to fine tune the optimum balance of skills and abilities. Some people may be fully trained in the skills they offer whilst others may be developing. Some may have the wisdom of the years on their side, others the vigour of youth, but all must contribute to the whole and a balance must be achieved. Research [2] has enabled us to understand why teams succeed or fail, by analysing the roles which are necessary in effective teams. Each of the following roles has its unique contribution to make.

THE LEADER

All teams need a leader, although members may assume the role of leader in different situations. At the outset, the leader's job is to form the team, to identify strengths and weaknesses, and to determine the scope of wanted contributions. Objectives must be set and performance monitored. Meetings will be called and a structure provided for them. The main contribution of the leader is to get the best out of everyone and to review the varied needs of the team at key stages of its development and for specialised tasks.

THE CHALLENGER

Often seen as the 'Maverick' of the team as he/she often adopts an unconventional approach. This is an individual who will look afresh at what the team is doing. He/she will challenge the accepted order. Because of this, such an individual is sometimes unpopular with those who prefer to conform. The challenger provides unexpected ideas and, whilst many of these may prove to be worthless, some may become 'the idea of the year'. Without a challenger the team can become complacent for it lacks the stimulus to review radically what the team is doing and how it is doing it.

THE EXPERT

We live in an age of ever increasing specialisation and the team may require several specialists whose primary role is to provide expertise which is not otherwise available to the team. Outside their area of specialisation, these members make little contribution; in meetings they assume the role of 'expert witness' giving a professional viewpoint which the rest of the team may need to evaluate in the light of other constraints and opportunities. The expert may be an accountant, engineer, marketing adviser, trainer, personnel specialist, corporate planner or any other specialist whose primary role is to provide the team with the expertise required to meet a particular objective.

THE AMBASSADOR

Like ambassadors who represent governments overseas, the ambassador in a team 'goes abroad' and builds the external relationships which enable the team to complete its task. An outgoing personality who makes friends easily, this is the public relations representative who tests the environment in which the team operates: a salesperson and a bridge builder who makes connections and knows the right people.

THE JUDGE

Like the judge in the courtroom this team member listens, questions and ponders before making a decision. This character tends to keep out of the arguments and does not see himself or herself as an advocate for any particular view or cause, but is concerned to see that ideas are properly evaluated and that sensible decisions are made.

A judge will not be rushed, preferring to pay the price of slow progress to make sure that the team follows the right path. Down to earth and logical, regarded by some as slow and ponderous, this person provides a balance and a check on those who may be carried away by their own enthusiasm, like the courtroom judge seeking out the truth and seeing justice done.

THE INNOVATOR

Here is the team member who uses imagination to the full: an ideas person who is always proposing new ways of doing things. The innovator ensures that new ideas are evaluated, nurtured and developed and builds on the original ideas of others, visualising opportunities and transforming ideas into practical strategies. A fearless capacity to grapple with complex problems which demand new approaches provides the team with a rich source of vision, ingenuity, imagination and logic and can usually help the team to understand with unconventional perspectives.

THE DIPLOMAT

The diplomat is the team member who knows the diplomatic solution. This character generally has high influence within the team and is a good negotiator, and because of these skills plays a large part in orientating the team towards successful outcomes. Building alliances within and outside the team and trying to ensure that solutions are acceptable to all, the diplomat can sometimes be accused of 'papering over the cracks' in an effort to compromise, but is often dealing with the 'art of the possible' rather than the ideal solution. Ways are found through difficult problems, and in difficult times this is often the person who leads the team through dangerous ground.

THE CONFORMER

Helping in every way and always to be relied upon to fill the inevitable gap that no-one had thought of, the conformer adopts a co-operative stance and so helps the others to feel at ease. This character seldom challenges authority, rarely rocks the boat, preferring to use time and skills to good effect. Often the team's odd-job person who may not have any outstanding expertise, but he/she observes what is happening and what is needed and then uses a breadth of experience to its best advantage. Invaluable as a 'fixer', he or she works for the good of the team and is generally conservative in outlook.

THE OUTPUT DRIVER

A self motivated achiever with persistent drive to see tangible results, this is the team's target person who reminds everyone about time scales and output requirements, who acts as the progress chaser and ensures that the team 'gets to its target'. He or she has high task commitment and this can rub off on others, ensuring a more results orientated operation. This character is often intolerant of the views and problems of other team members and can be abrasive in approach.

THE QUALITY CONTROLLER

Here is a check on the 'output orientation' of the output driver. The quality controller is often heard to remark 'If a job is worth doing it is worth doing well'. Quality is the watchword. This is the person who inspires the team to strive for higher standards, who can be accused of holding up progress and who may often clash with the output driver in the desire to see that quality is maintained. Here is the conscience of the team, upholding concern for the quality of relationships, services and leadership as well as the product itself.

THE SUPPORTER

The supporter makes people feel at ease and builds morale within the team. This character is strongly relationships orientated, seeking to ensure that the right conditions are created for people to give of their best and derive satisfaction from their working life. The supporter takes a lead in resolving conflict within the group but prefers to get to the root of the problem rather than paper over the cracks. Others feel that they can turn to the supporter for advice. This member of the team supports and encourages and hence is a considerable help in developing the contribution of others.

THE REVIEWER

Full of objective observations about the way in which the team is operating, this character helps the team to perform better in the future by reviewing past performance. Because it is easier to observe from the outside whilst not taking part in a task, part of this role can on occasions be given to an external consultant who specialises in 'process review'. However, this is not a substitute for the regular internal review which is a hallmark of highly successful teams. The reviewer gives feedback to the team, acting as a mirror and enabling the team to see itself, looks for pitfalls and continually considers the way in which the team operates, tends to be a sceptic and is 'process' rather than 'task' or 'relationships' orientated.

Remember that each of the above is a role and not an individual member. Some individuals may act almost exclusively in one of the roles but others may represent a blend of roles. Perhaps the most useful member of any team is one who can adopt different roles in different situations. Obviously the smaller the team the more roles it is necessary for each member to play.

2 CLEAR OBJECTIVES AND AGREED GOALS

A senior management team were holding their first 'clear the air' session. The topic under discussion was deadlines for financial information. The accountant was saying how irritated he was with the way that people failed to provide the necessary data at specified times. Then somcone asked him 'Why do you need this information?' He replied, 'For management information.' Then the accountant was asked, 'Who uses the information?' He replied, 'Well this team needs the information.' The team looked disbelieving then broke into laughter, and one team member said, 'For two years I believed that this information was for someone else and now I realise that it is for us. In that case, I'll do it on time and I've got some things to say about how it can be made more useful.'

Only when the objective of an activity becomes clear is it possible for people to pull together constructively and decide what is relevant and important. Many organisations demonstrate from their daily functioning that clear objectives are absent. We frequently see unhealthy competition between groups and individuals pursuing their personal goals at the expense of others.

Simply acquiring a clear definition of an objective is only a small part of the story. Until objectives are agreed they have little force. The process of agreeing objectives is frequently tedious and lengthy as apparently irrelevant objections are brought up and need to be worked through. Often people need to reconcile their own views and objectives with those of the wider organisation and this can be a difficult task. For example, we know of one person who held a responsible job as a research officer before contracting an illness which sapped her strength for years. Although she could continue to work it became her personal objective to limit her involvement so as to avoid excessive strain. The team to which she belonged, however, had different objectives where were concerned with increasing effectiveness and maximising output. In this case it became necessary to view the conflict between personal and team objectives so that creative solutions could be found to maintain team performance without undermining a team member's health.

It is a vain hope to imagine that every member of a team can be fully committed to identical objectives. Differences of opinion and conflicting interests will always exist and the most significant requirement is to develop mechanisms for exploring viewpoints, finding common ground and learning to live with differences.

Senior groups often begin a teambuilding programme with the intention of working on clarifying their objectives. The pressures on such groups can be extreme; as one manager said, 'When the alligators are snapping at your hindquarters it is hard to realise that your job is to drain the swamp.' In a complex environment where many variables remain unknown, objectives can be difficult to specify and many factors change rapidly. This places additional emphasis on the importance of team skill in setting objectives. Undeveloped teams lack the capacity to work together to take opportunities and clarify objectives in a difficult and confusing environment.

Some of the main barriers to clear objective-setting are:

1. A tendency to judge performance on the basis of personal opinion rather than measured output. People are often judged on the basis of their appearance, impact on others, attitudes, and even sex appeal. When the criteria for success are clearly identified in relation to the output and judgements are clearly related to results, then thinking in terms of objectives becomes relevant and widely practised.
2. Lack of skills in objective-setting. It has been widely known for decades that objectives should, as far as possible, be (a) specific, (b) time bound and (c)

101

measurable. Nevertheless, when managers set objectives they frequently produce vague intentions more in keeping with new year resolutions than business goals.

3. Insufficient tenacity in adhering to objectives. Interruptions and unforeseen events constantly occur and new priorities become important. Unless a firm stance is taken urgent but relatively trivial matters undermine progress towards agreed objectives.

4. Undertaking irrelevant tasks. It is sometimes easy to set an objective and then discover later that little benefit has come from effort expended. When setting a task it is helpful to ask the question 'Why?', which leads to deciding whether the objective is significant and relevant. Only when objectives can be seen to be useful should they be accepted as guidelines.

When a team possesses a clearly stated set of objectives to which all members feel committed it has achieved a great deal. Greater motivation, fewer demands on management, better problem-solving and more initiatives are the desirable outcomes of clear objectives and agreed goals.

3   OPENNESS AND CONFRONTATION

Two managers were facing each other across a desk. One said, 'Henry, I really can't understand why you are so obstructive! I've asked you twenty times for that ADC 20 report and I'm still waiting. As it happens I've now got a copy through devious means.' Henry looked irritated and said, 'That's typical of you, Bill. Always going behind my back. I don't like the way that you demand everything and keep your hand close to your chest. The reason why I didn't give you the ADC 20 report is that it's not finished. You must have got the first draft.'

Their team manager was watching this exchange and he decided that the problem ought to be discussed in depth. He encouraged both men to speak their minds and describe how they saw each other. The discussion continued for half an hour as perceptions were exchanged and old wounds were brought out and displayed. At the end of the session both sat back in their chairs, sighed and grinned at each other. They knew that new difficulties would occur but had learned that they now had a greater capacity to work through difficulties and achieve constructive conclusions.

It is widely felt that conflict is a characteristic of an inadequate relationship and that mature individuals can always function together in harmony, and many people will do what they can to bury potential conflicts and inhibit their expression. Many see this as desirable because discomfort is avoided but, in reality, suppression of real conflict allows negative feelings to fester and causes a breakdown in real communication.

Teams which work well together are capable of coping with confrontation and encourage a high level of openness between team members. This quality of relationship needs to be built and reinforced by genuine feelings of support between team members. If a team is to be effective then its members need to feel able to state views, opinions, judgements, rational and irrational feelings, facts and hunches without fear of being belittled or embarrassed. Team relationships which diminish individual prestige or self-confidence result in attempts at self-protection and malicious sniping, which are real enemies of team effectiveness. When self-expression is inhibited there is often a considerable erosion of creativity and effort as more and more energy is invested in 'keeping heads down'. Effective teams are capable of tackling difficult, demanding or unpleasant issues in an open and problem-solving way.

The principles of developing openness and confrontation in a group are illustrated in the chart below:

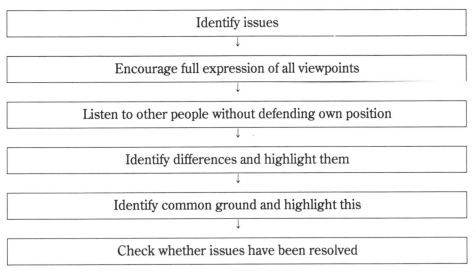

A high level of openness and confrontation is a characteristic of all mature relationships in all walks of life, but in working life it is not easy to achieve. Risks must be taken as people disclose information which may be contentious or may disturb the status quo. Real communication is direct, honest, and results in the development of genuine understanding of views and the sharing of experiences. One common source of inhibition is fear of the potential reaction of people with power in the team. The team manager often sets the standards of openness and confrontation, and his or her example is quickly identified and behaviour adjusted accordingly.

Openness and confrontation are partly stances to life and partly skills which can be learned. We can choose whether to disclose relevant information or withhold it. Our approach can also vary between 'straight' through 'withholding' to 'devious'.

Each approach has advantages and disadvantages which are summarised in Table 11.1.

Advantages	Disadvantages
Straight Trusted Authoritative Feels strong	Exposed Vulnerable Cannot delude Can be dull
Withholding Not exposed Difficult to attack Feels self satisfied	Frustrated Ineffective Uncreative
Devious Can delude Changes according to situation Exciting	Not trusted Builds resentment Can be ineffective Few friends

Table 11.1 Stances to Openness

Each person takes a personal stance towards openness, but in our experience team effectiveness is always enhanced by members deciding to be fully open – straight – and diminished by those who are withholding or devious.

The skills of openness and confrontation have much to do with 'assertion', 'active listening', and 'giving feedback'.

ASSERTION

The assertive person knows what he or she thinks and wants, takes definite and clear action to achieve goals and is unwilling to be side-tracked or easily defeated. Notice that we distinguish assertion from aggression which uses unfair force in an attempt to dominate. Assertion skills include clear presentation, dealing with one issue at a time, avoiding being undermined by others and seeking creative compromises. When all team members practise assertion skills there are plenty of ideas to evaluate, weak decisions are questioned and all viewpoints can be taken into account.

ACTIVE LISTENING

Openness and confrontation are usually associated with negative feelings and viewpoints. Of course this is not always the case as it is equally important to be open about positive judgements and expressions of personal warmth. However, whether negative or positive feelings are being expressed it often happens that they are not fully heard as the receiver fails to pay attention or allow him/herself to absorb what is being said. The skills of active listening can be learned, although many people find them difficult to acquire. These are the key characteristics of effective listeners:

1. They pay attention to what is being said.
2. They suspend judgement until they have heard the 'whole story'.
3. They look at the person who is talking.
4. They check that they understand what is being said.
5. They 'park' things in their minds and deal with them later.

Where a team practises listening skills when it meets there is a greater possibility of members openly expressing views without being prematurely judged. This leads to improved communication and a willingness to meet other people half way.

GIVING FEEDBACK

As a team develops it is inevitable that people will form views of each other and operate on the assumption that their opinions are objective. It is helpful for people to express their perceptions of each other and this process has become known as 'giving feedback'. The idea fills many people with alarm as they fear that the inevitable end result must be operational mayhem and psychological carnage. Experience suggests that the opposite is the case and giving feedback strengthens individuals, relationships and overall team identity. Feedback also leads people to question their assumptions about each other and develop more realistic and deeper relationships. Good feedback can be summarised as follows:

1. It is specific.
2. It is descriptive.
3. It clearly expresses views.
4. It is timed to be near the event being discussed.
5. It takes into account the needs of the receiver.
6. It is checked to ensure clear communication.
7. It concentrates on things the person can do something about.

When feedback is developed within a team, members can learn much from each other. Individuals who use feedback constructively have acquired a valuable asset. As team members learn to express their judgements and views they gain strength and release blocked energy. The team gains vitality and the individual grows in stature.

4 SUPPORT AND TRUST

A team of architects were congratulating themselves on the completion of a tender for a huge new bridge in the Middle East. The difficulties of design had tested their skills to the utmost but the tender was finally complete and in the envelope ready to go by special courier. One of the junior members seemed uncomfortable and distant. Then she said to the project leader, 'Tom, I'm worried about those calculations I did for the secondary supporting struts – will you check them?' The team manager said, 'Jean, you can't be serious! You are serious? What's the problem?' After analysis it turned out that a relatively unimportant error had been made but no alterations to the design were required. The tender was submitted within the deadline. Three months later the team were celebrating winning the contract and Jean, the junior architect, said to her manager, 'Tom, I want to thank you for not ripping me apart over that last-minute recalculation on the struts. I thought that you would go crazy, but I really appreciated the way that you didn't push me into the cesspit.' The manager said, 'Well, Jean, if you had kept it to yourself and the bridge had fallen down then we would all be locked in the cesspit for a hundred years.'

Support and trust are extremely valuable characteristics of human relationships. One of the reasons why so much business has historically been done between family relatives or within ethnic groups is that a high level of trust has been built up. Trust becomes a valuable commodity which enables risks to be taken that would otherwise be avoided.

Support has been defined as 'to strengthen by assistance'. This definition clearly makes the point that support is not a cosy and shallow sympathy but a genuine concern to assist the other person even if this involves giving negative feedback or facing difficult issues. It is possible to support a person without approving of everything that he or she does. Conflict avoided in the name of giving support is a short-sighted policy as such relationships are built on a false foundation of apparent warmth.

Trust usually takes a long time to develop and is not acquired easily as it is one of the deepest of human emotions. Trust takes time to build as it usually results from an accumulation of experiences through both good times and bad times. When we say that we trust another person we are not saying that we can predict what they will do, but we are usually able to predict their intentions. Our trust is that they will look after our interests and not consciously or unconsciously abuse us.

Support and trust go together as they are the bonds which link people in healthy relationships. A relationship of trust can be very vulnerable, as it can be destroyed by one malicious action or inhumane stance. Support is easier to feel but some people find it is harder to express because many social conventions inhibit the open expression of warmth.

Within a team context it is vital to develop a climate which encourages support and trust. Without support a high level of confrontation would be too harsh, whilst without trust individuals lack a willingness to disclose their true thoughts and feelings. As a team matures we see a gradual development of support and trust which are superficially present in the early stages but become deep only later in the process of team development. A fully developed team is a very close unit in which people are able to rely on each other sometimes even in matters of life or death.

Barriers to the development of support and trust are:

1. People are not trustworthy: Not everyone is trustworthy or capable of giving support. Some teams contain members whose personal development has not progressed enough for them to be trusted. Where there are such members it is necessary for the issues surrounding trust to be openly confronted and worked through.
2. Destructive competitive relationships: Where team members are seeking competitive advantage over each other, their relationships sometimes become characterised by showing off and point-scoring. Some lose out in the scramble for eminence and they feel second-rate citizens. People often feel very possessive and defensive about their areas of responsibility, even about the information they possess. Such competitiveness within the team can be very destructive to the development of relationships.
3. Withholding views: When people refuse to express their views, others make deductions about intentions and these are usually negative. The lack of willingness to be open reduces trust and undermines supportive relationships.
4. Imposition of Goals: When goals or standards are imposed, rather than agreed, this can easily be perceived as domineering, patronising or condescending and people feel resentful that they are being treated as mere resources rather than responsible human beings.

Within a team the qualities of high support and trust are greatly valued by members. Where these characteristics exist, then team members will tend to lay aside their sectional or personal interests and strive to make the team a satisfying and effective unit.

5 CO-OPERATION AND CONFLICT

A new manager was appointed to the engineering services team in a large chemical factory. He watched the team operate for a few weeks and then called them together. He said, 'I've been watching you for several weeks and I think that there is room for improvement. It is clear that you all like and respect each other and that you are prepared to say what you think. But I'll tell you what I've noticed – you don't go out of your way to help each other. You keep in your own domains and it seems to me that you could all co-operate much more.' The team were taken aback as they had always prided themselves on their working relationships, but when they discussed their work habits it became clear that they did regard each other as independent units and they could find opportunities for increased co-operation.

Co-operation can be expressed as 'working together for common gain'. This is an essential characteristic of a team approach, where the individuals put the team's objectives before their own and share in the gains and rewards from their joint activities. Co-operation implies that individuals are committed to work within a team and share their skills and information with other members. All teams require that their members devote time to forming and maintaining the health of the group. There is an element of sacrifice because each gives up some autonomy and self-interest. Committed team members feel that the goals and output of the team are important and personally satisfying. One test of team commitment is to explore how much enjoyment team members get from each other.

A mature team will pour its resources into helping a team member who is having difficulties. They will co-operate to help practically and give emotional support. A less committed team may watch a colleague in trouble with the dispassionate concern of an onlooker sitting knitting behind the guillotine during the French Revolution.

Co-operation begins when a team has clarified its goals and ensured that all its members feel that the objectives are both achievable and important. From here the team needs to develop mechanisms to enable team members to relate together during the decision-making and operational processes. Everyone is open about their need for help and about personal strengths and weaknesses. Team members watch each other's progress and are prepared to help if one member falls behind.

The team atmosphere encourages people to work with each other. Individuals listen to the ideas of others and build on them, seeking to make the best of what is available. Morale is improved as abilities, skills and experience are utilised by the team.

As co-operation increases, the team begins to learn how to use conflict constructively and positively. Conflict is often seen as a negative characteristic which should be suppressed and avoided. However, a mature team finds ways to channel conflicting ideas and viewpoints into a synthesis of ideas which has the best components of all opinions expressed. Positive conflict is exciting to experience and stimulating to the imagination. It destroys complacency and laziness as more truthful opinions are expressed.

Most teams which have demonstrated high creative capacity are able to use conflict as a tool for progress. The characteristics of these teams include:

1. Lack of rigid attitudes: a preparedness exists to consider different ideas and perceptions.
2. Clear presentation of ideas: divergent thoughts are clearly presented and fully expressed.
3. Open reactions: team members feel free to give their honest opinions directly and forcefully.
4. Techniques for conflict resolution: although conflict is encouraged, divergent ideas are related and common solutions identified.

Traditionally conflict has been seen as a negative characteristic promoted by trouble makers who are seeking personal acclaim at the expense of the team. Of course, destructive conflict is present in many relationships. However, the potential benefit from constructive conflict is great as it promotes more realistic and effective problem solving. Skills of conflict resolution can be learned and the procedures which follow are generally applicable.

A developed team has accomplished a high degree of co-operation which enables the resources of the group to be used for the benefit of all. When relationships do conflict, such differences are welcomed positively as they help bring creativity and realism to the group.

The main stages of conflict resolution are summarised in the following chart:

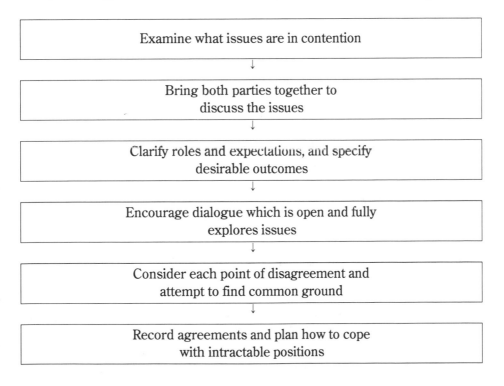

Examine what issues are in contention

↓

Bring both parties together to discuss the issues

↓

Clarify roles and expectations, and specify desirable outcomes

↓

Encourage dialogue which is open and fully explores issues

↓

Consider each point of disagreement and attempt to find common ground

↓

Record agreements and plan how to cope with intractable positions

6 SOUND PROCEDURES

John's team was highly regarded. People who belonged to the team felt proud to be associated with it. Relationships were excellent and morale was outstanding. One day John was called to his senior manager's office and the boss said, 'John, I want to discuss your team, it's just not delivering the goods.' John was outraged as he felt that his team leadership goals were a model to other managers. The senior manager continued, 'The morale is excellent but, John, you and your people are simply not good at solving problems. Have a look at it and come back to me.' After a thorough diagnosis it became apparent that the team lacked sound procedures for solving problems and getting things done.

Most teams consist of individuals who have different functional or specialist reponsibilities. The behaviour of each team member affects the others and procedures for clarifying roles, channelling communications and managing meetings need to be effective. It is helpful for members to discuss the team's basic organisation and assess whether their existing procedures are meeting the needs of the situation.

When a team meets together it needs to find answers to many questions and this demands good decision-making procedures and working relationships. The checklist below lists a number of crucial issues which need to be considered:

1. Is decision-making formal or informal?
2. Who has power and in what situations?
3. Are the people affected by decisions involved in the decision-making process?
4. How thorough is the information collection process?
5. Do we collect information quickly enough?
6. Are authority and responsibility matched when assignments are delegated?
7. How effectively are decisions communicated?
8. Are sufficient resources available?
9. Are resources co-ordinated?
10. Does the team set aside time to learn from experience?

Decision-making is a key aspect of the manager's job, yet the process is often done badly. Sometimes poor decision-making results from the lack of a planned systematic approach. One useful procedure for decision-making is the 'seven step approach'.

As its name implies, the seven step approach identifies seven key stages in decision-making. There is no simple format that can be mechanically applied to all problems and decisions and this approach is most useful when applied flexibly. The systematic approach is particularly useful when difficulties occur as it assists in identifying weaknesses in methodology.

SEVEN STEPS FOR STRUCTURED PROBLEM SOLVING AND DECISION-MAKING

Step One: Tuning In

The first requirement is to come to grips with the problem, assess its nature, understand the likely challenges and begin organising to cope with it. It is often helpful to try to identify an outline timescale and to identify whether unusual resources may be required. Each team member needs to understand the nature of the problem so that he or she can contribute fully to the decision-making process.

Step Two: Objective Setting

An objective is a statement of desired output. Sometimes objectives are clear and readily agreed, whilst on other occasions they are broad, hazy or contentious. An objective needs to be specific and understood by all before it can be achievable. Clarifying objectives is essential as it can prevent many of the misunderstandings and defensive arguments that result from some people not knowing what is happening.

Step Three: Success Criteria

Although objectives should be expressed in measurable terms it is useful to consider how you will monitor your progress. Two questions are useful:

1. How do we measure whether we have achieved the objective?
2. How do we judge whether we have worked together effectively?

When all concerned are aware of the methods of measuring success it becomes possible to use resources and time effectively. It is particularly important to identify success criteria when unspecific objectives are being tackled, so the statement 'to lose weight' becomes much more useful when it is stated as 'to lose one pound in weight each week for three months'.

Step Four: Information Collection and Decision Making

Most problems need to be understood in depth before a solution can be found. People have opinions, feelings, facts, ideas and prejudices to contribute. Certain kinds of problems may involve research or data collection outside the team. All of this information needs to be collected and made sense of to provide the basis for informed decision-making. Unfortunately, the human brain cannot work with too much data at any one time, so skilful techniques of displaying information greatly aid recognition of key issues and choices. When the necessary information has been collected different choices and options need to be identified and their merits explored.

Step Five: Planning

The planning stage begins with a decision about what is to be done. For example, in pursuit of the objective 'to make £25 000 by Christmas' we may have identified three options:

1. Become a tennis star.
2. Sell newspapers in the street.
or
3. Make a successful pop record.

The planning stage begins with our choice which may be to 'sell newspapers in the street'. Then we must decide:

1. What is to be done?
2. When is it to be done?
3. How is it to be done?
4. Where is it to be done?
5. What we need to do to make it happen?
6. How we are going to control it?

For action to be successful each person involved needs to be able to visualise clearly what is to be done and to identify his or her role.

Step Six: Action

It has been said that there is no substitute for getting things done. Most decisions are taken because something needs to happen differently. If all the preceding five stages have been thoroughly undertaken the team will have the best chance of achieving a successful outcome. The quality of performance is largely a function of the quality of preparation with, perhaps, a little bit of luck thrown in for good measure.

Step Seven: Review to Improve

We learn from seeing the results of our actions. As we examine the factors which led to success and failure we have a most valuable opportunity for learning and personal growth. Accordingly, the final stage of a systematic problem-solving and decision-making cycle is deliberately to set aside time to review performance with the intention of learning from the experience. It is important to avoid becoming dispirited or pessimistic as sometimes the most disastrous happenings provide us with highly significant learning. Without feedback there is little chance of changing and developing.

At certain times in the decision-making cycle the group may choose to use a consensus approach to pool the maximum number of ideas and gain maximum commitment. Consensus is a difficult approach to decision-making. At best it offers an excellent opportunity to collect ideas, clarify objectives and plan coherent action. At worst, consensus-seeking is an excuse for muddled decision-making and poor morale.

Here are some guidelines which may help you to improve the quality of consensus groups:

1. Ground rules:

- identify basic ground rules
- stress importance of reasoning
- avoid people arguing for their own views at expense of group
- seek to identify logic

2. Individual positions:

- ask people to clarify their 'going-in' positions
- be explicit about assumptions
- clarify where each person stands

3. Clarify objectives:

- try to explore objectives
- work hard to share objectives
- record statement of objectives

4. Handling information:

- use a visual display of data
- try to visualise suggestions to test them
- explore understanding of the problem

5. Listening:

- try to hear each other
- avoid over-talking
- avoid premature judgement

6. Assertion:

- help less assertive people
- be intolerant of aggression
- avoid being sidetracked
- clearly state views

7. Co-ordination:

- leader must be skilful
- periodic summaries help
- leader organises group to tackle problem

8. If you get stuck:

- try reviewing objectives
- clarify issue in dispute
- assemble data
- try to make most probable deduction
- collect new data if necessary

The team leader is the key man in determining the degree to which the team will participate in decision-making. There are four basic approaches which can be used:

1. I take the decisions: the leader retains control and feels no obligation to consult.
2. I will seek your opinion and then decide: the leader makes the decisions after discussing the topic with team members.
3. I will choose others to help me in taking decisions: the leader selects others to assist him or her in decision-making.
4. We will take decisions: the problem is brought before the team who discuss it and jointly solve the problem.

Effective decision-making in teams requires sound information handling, communication and skilful problem-solving. It is important that procedures are reviewed and challenged from time to time as they can become fossilised. The team must continue to seek simple and effective procedures that enable the maximum return from available resources.

7 APPROPRIATE LEADERSHIP

An American enterprise engaged in the micro-chip business having expanded rapidly had decided to open an office in Europe. The marketing vice-president commissioned an extensive survey and judged that Hamburg would be the best location. He joined the corporation president for a planning meeting and found the chief executive reading his report. The president said, 'I like the concept, Hal, but why Hamburg?' The marketing vice-president replied, 'To me the logic suggests that Hamburg will be the most convenient location.' The president sat back in his chair and said, 'Well, my philosophy is to give a man his head. Some people will make it work from a hut in Tahiti whilst others will fail even though they have all the resources imaginable. First choose the man and then find the location. Of course, it has to be sensible, but if you get the right guy to head it up, then he'll make it work.'

The president was talking about leadership, which is a crucial quality in organisational life. An effective leader makes best use of resources and develops competence and capability. An ineffective leader squanders potential and misplaces effort. Organisational effectiveness depends greatly on the quality of leadership.

In recent years we have begun to understand leadership behaviour more clearly. It was apparent that some individuals were excellent leaders in one situation but completely unable to cope in a different context. We can now identify with precision the skills of leadership and when a particular kind of leadership is appropriate.

Studies of leadership have determined that leaders perform two vital functions: whilst influencing people in what to do and controlling situations, they develop good relationships and encourage participation.

It has been shown that people need different kinds of leadership according to their ability and attitude. When there is low availability or low willingness to perform a task it is necessary for the leader to spend a lot of time in controlling and directing. However, where there is greater ability and willingness to perform, a leader will encourage individuals by increasing participation and involvement.

Studies have shown that always the most important factor was the character of the group or individual being led. It seemed that a style of management would work well in one setting but not in another. In other words there was no single best approach which could be used universally. The leader who used an appropriate style for a particular group was the person who would most often succeed in achieving high output.

Other studies have tried to analyse situations to see whether it was possible to identify key characteristics. Work by two Americans, Paul Hersey and Kenneth Blanchard[3], took this much further. These two researchers hit upon the idea of relating style to the degree to which subordinates were capable and felt comfortable about tackling the job in hand. This measurement of 'maturity' could be carried out quite scientifically; at the lowest level it was defined as unwilling and unable, whilst the most mature people were defined as willing and able.

Linking these two ideas together, it became apparent that the manager dealing with an unwilling and unable group needs to spend a lot of time clarifying goals and simply telling people what needs to be done. ('Telling')

As the group develops, so they require to get to know him or her as a person, and become interested in the work and the people around them. ('Selling')

Later, as they become more mature, so the wish for participation and involvement grows. The group can be left much more to tend to their own affairs. They still need help and direction, but not the same energy or control which was present earlier. They have grown beyond this. ('Participating')

At the fourth stage, group members are largely self-directed, as they organise their own affairs. Here the management style appropriate to the situation is characterised by delegation. The manager can trust his or her subordinates to get on with the problem in hand. This leaves time to tackle other jobs, such as planning and representing the group outside. ('Delegating')

Teams go through a number of development stages and the effective leader helps the group progress to a high level of responsibility and competence. This means that he or she needs:

● to know where the team is at the moment
● to know how the team is likely to progress
● to know what he or she can do to help

Teams can be viewed as being in one of these four positions:

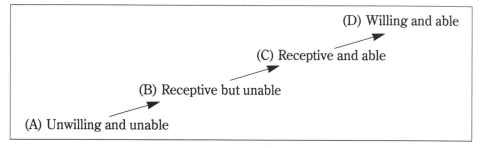

Teams develop slowly and can lapse. However, almost all can be helped and encouraged to progress to a higher level of maturity. As control and instruction are decreased, so the behaviour of the group needs to be watched to see that they take responsibility and perform well. The diagram below shows the process.

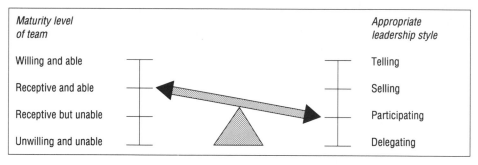

Fig. 11.1 The Leadership Style Balance

Gradually, the balance shifts as the team becomes more responsible and capable. Ultimately, the team becomes capable of handling its own internal management and problems.

Not all teams need leaders of a permanent nature, as many mature teams are able to change their leadership to suit circumstances. High team maturity can be judged by such things as:

● high level of achievement
● open and friendly relations between team members
● capacity to undertake assignments without help
● shrewd use of available resources

- capacity to deal with uncertainty
- rapid reaction to new circumstances
- high level of energy
- good mix of individual skills and personalities
- effective problem solving procedures.

With the development of team competence it becomes possible for the team manager to delegate important areas of responsibility. Delegation is not only a way of enabling a manager to devote more time to other issues; it is also recognition of the ability and maturity of others. Often a low level of delegation results from lack of trust in subordinates, insufficient time spent in training and development activities and excessive involvement with the hectic but trivial events of the moment. Delegation should enhance rather than threaten the manager's status. Any manager who claims that he is indispensable should question whether he is now avoiding developing his subordinates to their full potential.

Delegation can be defined as 'passing responsibility for the completion of tasks downwards'. However, the person to whom work is delegated must have sufficient initiative to change course, according to circumstances. Simply telling someone to undertake a task is not real delegation as genuine discretion has to be exercised.

Many managers find it difficult to delegate as they fear that important aspects of the job will be neglected or bungled. However, the benefits are clear:

- less strain on the manager
- better use of team resources
- genuine development of subordinates
- quicker decision-making
- better use of time
- more creativity
- improvement in morale.

Despite the potential pitfalls, the case for delegation is overwhelming. It could be described as the ultimate style of leadership where work is being completed without the need for control or support.

Effective delegation is based on the following principles:

1. An analysis of areas of accountability and identification of tasks that can be delegated.
2. Consideration of the present maturity level of each team member and training to develop their competence.
3. Progressive assignment of tasks to build a more responsible work load.
4. Regular counselling and review.
5. Emphasis on clarifying objectives and establishing success criteria.

There are often risks in delegation, but if these are intelligently managed the leader reaps high rewards.

Effective leadership is essential for the development of teamwork. When a team leader lacks the ability or skills to develop a team approach it is probable that the potential of the group will never be exploited. One of the most important leadership functions is to provide opportunities for important issues to be clarified and worked through to a satisfactory resolution. Teams grow in stature as they confront issues and deal with them. This can be done by setting a personal example, demonstrating openness in practice. Once barriers have been broken through, the release of energy and greater depth of relationships more than outweigh any discomfort experienced. Individuals are brought together, objectives clarified, relationships built in a confronting yet supportive climate, and satisfying and effective work methods developed. The most respected leaders are those who are authentic because it is almost always disastrous to 'play a leadership role' rather than be oneself.

The effective team leader:

- is in touch with his own energy and stimulates others
- has studied team development and can aid his group progress
- adopts an open approach which builds trust
- develops an authentic style
- affirms a positive view of human nature
- is clear about the standards he wishes to achieve
- is receptive to people's hopes, fears, problems and dignity
- faces facts honestly and squarely
- tries to make the work place happy, satisfying and interesting

8 REGULAR REVIEW

A group of senior managers were reviewing how they could communicate reorganisation plans to a workforce of thousands. They knew that many would feel threatened or angry by the inevitable changes, and they wanted to put a clear and convincing case to each employee. In the end it was decided that a special video film would be made which would be shown in every factory and office. Senior managers gathered in a studio and made their presentations to the video cameras. They immediately went and watched their efforts and at the end of the viewing the chief executive said, 'We've got to do a lot better than that. It's boring and confusing. Let's analyse where we are going wrong and try again.' They repeated this cycle four times and ultimately were satisfied. The film was seen by every company employee and the reorganisation plans were accepted.

Regular review of performance is essential to the development of competence. Sports teams are well aware of the need for review and spend hours discussing their successes and failures. They identify strengths and weaknesses and plan strategies for improvement.

The most valuable reviews incorporate objective and impartial data. A team will gain from periodic reflection on its performance and a dispassionate enquiry into missed opportunities and inadequate performance. Some teams appear to operate an informal conspiracy to avoid self-reflection and review. There are several possible reasons for this reluctance to review:

1. Politeness: team members feel that it is not appropriate to make personal comments about each other.
2. Fear of hurting others: concern that negative criticism may be damaging.
3. Lack of trust: the team lacks positive relationships which permit frank exchange.
4. Protection of the status quo: a belief that existing successes may be damaged by open criticism.
5. Poor skills: team members lack skills in self expression and analysis.

Regular review helps a team to evolve towards maturity. Usually we find that teams spend far too little time reviewing their effectiveness. It is often easy for each team meeting to finish with a review of effectiveness, and perhaps with regular teambuilding sessions, looking at broader aspects of team functioning.

There are many different approaches and aids to team review and once the skills of review are learned they become part of the way of life of the team. Here are some key techniques which have proved useful in practice.

USING AN OBSERVER

A team will often benefit from using an impartial observer who sits outside of the group. Often he will have a check list which helps him to analyse behaviour and give feedback to the group. He is really looking for those acts or words which helped the team in its task and those which hindered the achievement of objectives. The observer will be careful to avoid forming judgements and colouring the facts with his own prejudices. At a suitable point, the observer will be invited to report to the group and his or her comments will then form the basis of a discussion.

USING CLOSED-CIRCUIT TELEVISION

In the hands of someone who is both a skilled observer and a skilled operator of CCTV equipment, the video tape can be a most useful tool. The group can replay sections of its own activity and analyse in depth what happened and why. All are able to see for themselves how they behaved and each individual can assess his or her personal contribution to team effectiveness. In this way learning can be greatly speeded up and difficult issues identified, confronted and worked through.

USING TEAM SURVEYS

A wide range of team surveys are available to enable a team to monitor its own performance and set goals for its improvement. It is helpful for the team to identify potential weaknesses and devise a method for systematic review. Objectives can then be established for the improvement of performance and regular checks made on team effectiveness. Regular review has the following benefits:

- ensures that adequate effort is directed towards planning
- decision-making processes are improved
- support, trust and openness increase
- individuals improve their contributions
- meetings become more productive and enjoyable
- involvement and commitment increase.

The process of review is a vital stage in developing team effectiveness, yet we often see this step omitted as the pressures of daily life keep the team in a frenzy of activity. In the long term, however, time must be found to step back and consider the team's behaviour with an impartial but critical eye.

9 INDIVIDUAL DEVELOPMENT

A group of hospital administrators were facing a difficult dilemma. They were suffering from a shortage of money and staff and had to reduce the quality of care given to patients. All those present in the meeting had views about where they felt that economies could be made. One man, responsible for technical equipment, contributed little to the discussion, and gradually it was decided that his department should bear the brunt of the financial economies. The meeting was concluded and most of the managers left feeling satisfied. The technical manager, however, said to a colleague, 'You know, Tom, I feel badly about this. We've got our priorities all wrong. My department is taking far too big a share of the economies.' His colleague asked, 'Why didn't you speak out?' After a long pause the reply came, 'I don't know, I guess I'm poor at expressing myself.'

The team which allowed the manager to contribute poorly to the team on that occasion could be described as underdeveloped. The purpose of teamwork is to pool the skills of individuals and so produce a better result than that which individuals could achieve. The effectiveness of a team should be greater than the sum of its parts but, of course, teams need to pay attention to the development of individual skills and abilities, because these are the raw materials. When a person contributes weakly, the overall output of the team is diminished.

Individual development is a fascinating topic and our analysis[4] of individual capacity has identified eleven key problems or 'blockages', widely experienced by those in management jobs. These are:

120

1. Self-management incompetence: being unable to make the most of one's time, energy and skill or being unable to cope with the stresses of present day managerial life.
2. Unclear personal values: being unclear about one's own values or having values which are inappropriate to working and private life in the 1990s.
3. Confused personal goals: being unclear about one's personal life or work goals or having goals which are incompatible with work and life in the 1990s.
4. Stunted personal development: lacking the stance, ability and receptiveness to rise to new challenges and opportunities.
5. Inadequate problem solving skills: lacking the problem solving and decision making strategies and abilities necessary to solve the problems of the 1990s.
6. Low creativity: lacking the ability to generate sufficient new ideas to keep ahead, or to capitalise on them.
7. Low influence: having insufficient influence to gain commitment and help from others or to affect their decisions.
8. Lack of managerial insight: having insufficient understanding of the motivation of people at work or having values about the leadership of others which are out-dated, inhumane or inappropriate.
9. Poor supervisory skills: lacking the practical ability to achieve results through the efforts of others.
10. Low trainer ability: lacking the ability or willingness to help others to grow and expand their capacity.
11. Low teambuilding ability: being unable to help groups or teams to develop and become more effective.

When new members join a team it is important that they are introduced with understanding but also made to realise that high standards of performance are expected. A well-developed team member is one who:

- listens to others
- learns from experience
- is prepared to be open about his or her position
- will change a viewpoint through reason but not through bullying
- is willing to take reasonable risks
- develops good relations with others
- has sufficient personal energy
- assertively presents his or her case.

Individual development needs to be much more comprehensive than many conventional management textbooks suggest.

Business life is full of countless examples of executives who seem to have all the right skills and all the knowledge, technical and otherwise, and yet still never seem to achieve worthwhile results. We also meet many executives, particularly owner-managers who have had little training and on the surface appear deficient in the accepted managerial skills, and yet they have created immensely successful businesses and seem to have the knack of always succeeding.

In practice, management is about seeing opportunities, seizing them and making things happen, and some people seem able to do that continually. Observers have noticed that the most effective and the least effective almost invariably display two different sets of characteristics.

The less effective seem to have a passive approach to life wishing to be undisturbed as much as possible. They find challenge frightening and avoid it whenever possible. They also avoid insight into themselves and their beliefs. They do not welcome feedback from others and criticism, far from being perceived as healthy, is seen as unhelpful and threatening. They are not in touch with their own feelings, and do not wish to be, and new experiences are avoided because of the threat which they could bring. Often they try to manipulate people and seldom do they seek to increase the freedom of others. They lack concern for others and whilst they may give sympathy to them they rarely offer real help. Their beliefs are the beliefs of others, often learned in childhood and seldom seriously questioned; they are not authentic people. They are intolerant of divergent views and are often heard to bemoan the fact that others are not like them. In their unrelaxed posture towards life they are content with low standards. When difficult problems arise they are the first to shun responsibility. For them life would be happier if they were surrounded by weak people, but they are not and so they often resent the strong whom they see as contributing substantially to their unhappy and unsatisfactory lives.

Successful people by contrast seem to have an active approach to life. They are the people who make things happen and are constantly seeking new challenges for themselves and the groups which they represent. They wish to know more about themselves and are interested in the feedback which others can give them about both their strengths and their weaknesses. They welcome constructive criticism. They recognise that time and energy are limited in terms of human existence and, seeing them as man's most valuable resources, they plan their lives to make the most of them. They constantly seek new experiences because they see the quality of life being linked to an expanding range of experience. By constantly achieving good results they build a reputation as people who can be relied upon to 'come up with the goods', and they are committed to seeing things through even when difficult situations arise. They understand their own feelings and try to use them as a positive force in their relationships with others. They care about others and their feelings and whilst they may not always agree they remain tolerant to the beliefs of those around them. They strive to be open with others, for they have nothing to hide and they realise that honesty is a much neglected value but is usually the best course. They are not frightened to give freedom to others, realising that this is vital for personal growth. They set high standards for themselves and the groups which they represent and are constantly seeking opportunities to extend themselves and their colleagues. Because they have worked things through for themselves they are clear about their own beliefs and are not inhibited by the teachings of others. Because they are successful they are strong and they rejoice in that strength, using it as a positive force for themselves and their colleagues. They are relaxed, happy people who see life as an adventure which they enjoy immensely.

Very few people conform totally with either of these sets of characteristics; it is a question of degree, and individual development is essentially about which set of characteristics we move towards and which we move away from. The two sets of characteristics when placed side by side become stark alternatives: choices which we are able to make about ourselves, our approach to life and our approach to work. Often those individuals who predominantly exhibit the high effectiveness characteristics are uncomfortable people to work with, their drive and dynamism at first sight appearing to inhibit the common good of the team. The really effective teams, however, learn to capitalise on these qualities and encourage their less effective members to move towards them.

10   SOUND INTER-GROUP RELATIONS

A medium sized company had developed two sales teams. One, 'Dawnfresh Products', sold fresh vegetables to hotels and hospitals whilst the second, 'Dawnfresh Retail', serviced many thousands of small shops. Between these two groups a rivalry developed which gradually poisoned their relationship and co-operation. Each saw the other as arrogant, selfish and negative. The sales director watched the deterioration of this relationship and decided that it was damaging the effectiveness of his function. After discussion with a consultant it was decided to bring both groups together and try to 'lance the boil'. The day came and both teams sat looking at each other. The consultant suggested that each group, privately, select ten adjectives which they considered described the other group. Ten minutes were allowed for this task. When the lists were shared there was a stunned silence. Both groups were annoyed by the vehemence and hostility shown by the other team's adjectives. They began a furious exchange, and months of pent-up aggression were expressed. Gradually the excitement cooled and the groups were more able to look at their relationship from a realistic and balanced perspective. Finally they agreed to try to co-operate more and made plans to communicate more openly, and then they retired together to the bar for a few drinks.

Groups frequently develop inaccurate or negative views about each other. This can often be seen vividly between communities, as in the early 1990s in the case of Protestants and Catholics in Northern Ireland, or with the warring factions in the former Yugoslavia. Each develops a mental picture of the other and forms judgements about qualities and merit. Such perceptions often prejudice open and constructive relationships. If we look at the behaviour of early man when hunting bands and tribal loyalties governed relationships, then we can perhaps see how we learned to be suspicious of members of other groups, and developed the habit of strengthening our own group at the expense of others.

A small enterprise, in the pioneer stage, may function as a single team. However, with the growth of organisation, functional teams form, rather like cells dividing, to form a more complex organism. At this stage of development the senior team will seek to clarify overall objectives, but may well find that separate teams are unwilling to communicate or co-operate fully.

Inter-team relations often need to be consciously developed particularly where daily routines fail to provide sufficient contact to establish a rapport. Many managers fail to perceive the need for deliberate 'bridge building' between groups but usually much can be done to improve co-operation.

Inter-team relations are an important area because almost always teams need to co-operate together to achieve common objectives. Whilst it often seems that there is a natural force pulling a team together, it also often appears that there is an equally natural force which polarises teams. Indeed, some teams develop increased coherence by demonstrating their superiority above other groups. This has many negative effects for the wider organisation.

Groups frequently engage in negative competition which can be observed as a subtle undercurrent, expressed through negative comments, sarcastic remarks and the absence of open communication. Managers often talk about their jobs in terms borrowed from sport. They talk of 'scoring points', 'playing to win' and 'knowing the rules of the game'. Such expressions indicate how some team leaders think about their jobs. The images of 'winning' which we learn as children usually persist into adult life. So we may see one team succeeding whilst another fails. Teams rarely develop a real depth of communication with other teams.

The key symptoms of poor inter-group relations are:

- negative attitudes and 'sniping'
- little co-operative contact
- ponderous project work
- personalities unknown to others
- lack of shared objectives
- superior attitudes and destructive rivalry

Psychological studies using the transactional analysis framework observe many 'games' and destructive strategies between teams. For example, it is not unknown for one team deliberately to cause another team to lose face by playing 'Now I've got you, you son of a bitch'.[5]

There are ways to improve inter-group relations which can be undertaken by any manager in the daily routines of his job. These suggestions may appear mundane, but they frequently result in tangible benefit:

1. Ensure that the actions and decisions of the team are communicated and understood.
2. Recognise that although teams are not the same that is no reason for them to stay apart.
3. Try to understand the other team's point of view, recognising their problems and difficulties and offering a hand of friendship when needed.
4. Continually seek out ways of working effectively with others.
5. Don't be too rigid in defending team boundaries.
6. Recognise that boundaries and responsibilities between teams will need to be reviewed and amended from time to time.
7. Anticipate and eliminate potential inter-team problems before they arise.
8. Really try to listen to others and do all that is possible to help them listen to you.
9. Use others as a source of ideas and comparison.
10. Understand and utilise differences in people.
11. Make a point of joining the other team members for lunch/drinks.
12. Take active steps to find out what other teams do.
13. Hold periodic liaison meetings.
14. Try to find opportunities to help other teams in practical ways.
15. Make requests for help or information clearly and specifically.

One simple but useful technique for improving inter-group relations is called 'role negotiation'. Each team produces a written answer under four headings:

1. What things we would like you to do more or do better.
2. What things we would like you to do less or stop doing.
3. What things we would like you to begin to do that you do not do now.
4. What things you do which we would like to continue.

The teams share these lists and begin to discuss how their co-operation can be improved.

Once achieved, effective inter-group relationships bring a host of advantages. Amongst the foremost of these are greater ability to influence the organisation, more available help, easier flow of information, easier problem solving, less anxiety and happier, more enjoyable working lives.

Inter-group relations improve over time. Once a good rapport is established people tend to enjoy contact and find ways to increase co-operation and interaction. The basic characteristics of good inter-team relations are similar to those within a good team. In particular, trust, openness, confrontation and sound procedures are extremely important. In addition, it is important for each team to understand not only its own role within the wider organisation but also the roles of other teams. Sound inter-group relations build a supportive climate between groups, pull divergent threads together and increase overall effectiveness.

11 GOOD COMMUNICATIONS

Communication is the oil for the machinery. Or to select another metaphor, it is the power train linking the engine to the drive wheels.

Probably the most heard complaint in any organisation is that 'our communications are poor'. Ask any group of employees and you will almost invariably get the same answer, 'Our communications are in need of improvement'. This is not surprising if we consider the complexity of the pattern of communications in organisations. Effective communication is necessary at and between every level in an organisation, between its constituent parts and with many groups which comprise the external environment.

Each needs to communicate to some extent with the other, and depending upon the role most need to communicate with the external environment. Within an organisation, as problems become more and more complex, there is an increasing need for complex solutions which utilise the abilities of greater numbers of people often cutting across traditional hierarchical relationships.

COMMUNICATIONS WITHIN THE TEAM

Within the effective team, good communication is necessary between members with the same specialisations. For example, within teams there may be:

- managers who direct, control and co-ordinate
- operators who perform the central task
- analysts who innovate and rationalise
- support staff who enable the central task to be performed

All need to communicate with the others both as individuals and sub-groups.
Communications within the team can be enhanced by:

- improving the communications skills of individual team members
- facilitating a better flow of information and ideas

THE SKILLED COMMUNICATOR

As we examine people who consistently communicate well we can identify the requirements of the skilled communicator.

First of all the communicator will have a well developed sense of how his or her views, attitudes and actions impact on others. Personal strengths and weaknesses will be known. In short, he/she will have self knowledge.

Sureness of beliefs and values and honesty in dealings with others are important. As Shakespeare's Polonius put it, 'To thine own self be true, And it must follow as the night the day, Thou canst not then be false to any man'.

An ability to deal with all types of people in differing situations, the capacity to be flexible in approach according to need, are a mark of the communicator with interpersonal skills.

This person will be a good listener, actively listening and trying to 'hear' what others are really saying. As John Dunne said, 'There are those who listen and there are those who wait to talk'.

A manager, supervisor or a leader of a sub-group will have the ability to attune his leadership style to meet the needs of those being led, recognising that different people and different tasks require differing approaches from those who lead. This is leadership flexibility.

A communicator is a person who is perceived by others as 'worth listening to'. People will take notice of views when a person is seen to stand up for beliefs and if necessary to fight for them. Opposition will not cower such a person, whose assertiveness and presence will cope with any situation.

This person will recognise that often communication requires learning and that what is to be communicated to others may not be readily understandable by them. A willingness and ability to help others learn presuppose training and counselling skills.

This person will be able to communicate in the written word as well as face to face and will, therefore, require writing skills.

To stand up in front of a group and put a case over well and professionally will need presentation skills.

Because there may be a need to bring together people with differing viewpoints and contributions and utilise the whole of what they have to offer, he or she will have to be a competent Chairperson.

Overall, sensitivity to the needs, feelings and perceptions of others and an understanding of relationship requirements as well as task requirements are expected. The communicator will have sensitivity.

Some of these requirements are skills which can be learned through formal training sessions. Others are personal attributes which, whilst training can help, are more difficult to acquire, being the product of the kind of person that we are. Development of these requirements is more a question of personal questioning and experiment.

FACILITATING BETTER COMMUNICATIONS

Often communications within a team can be improved by making relatively minor changes in working practices, but some improvements require more fundamental work with team members. The following are all actions which can be initiated or developed to improve communications:

1. Attitude surveys: these can throw new light on how team members are feeling and what the barriers to better communications are.

2. Appraisal/counselling: either a formal or informal system can greatly improve willingness and ability to communicate.
3. Mass communications: using works newspapers, notice boards, bulletins, books and manuals, and so on, to get the message over.
4. Cascading: using the differing levels of management to 'cascade' information down and up the team.
5. Getting to know others: often people can work together for years without really knowing their colleagues. Activities and training sessions can be used to develop and open up relationships.
6. Works representatives: works councils and other employee representative groups, even trades unions, can be used to get the message across, although there are dangers in using agencies 'outside the team' to communicate information which is generated within the team.
7. Systematic planning: often people are reluctant to be a part of the action because they have not been part of the planning process which has gone before. Involvement at the planning stage encourages free communication at the action stage.
8. Working environment: often the mere layout of desks or workstations inhibits free communication. Ask how necessary separate offices/workrooms really are and whether they are acting as a barrier to communications. Territorial barriers are barriers to communication.
9. Eliminating unearned status symbols: seniority and status should be based on ability and contribution. Status symbols which are not perceived to be fully earned inhibit communication.
10. Value clarification: people will communicate better when they share a common perception of what the team stands for.

NOTES

[1] Janis, I.L., *Groupthink: Psychological Studies of Policy Decisions*, Houghton Mufflin, Boston, 1982.
[2] Belbin, M., *Management Teams – Why They Succeed and Fail*, Heinemann, London, 1981.
[3] Hersey, P. and Blanchard, K. H., *Management of Organisational Behaviour and Utilising Human Resources*, Prentice Hall, 1977.
[4] Woodcock, M. and Francis, D., *The Unblocked Manager*, Gower, Aldershot, 1982.
[5] Berne, E., *Games People Play: The Psychology of Human Relationships*, Grove Press Inc., 1964; André Deutsch, 1966.

12 Practical Teambuilding – A Guide to Resources

These then are the raw materials or building blocks which can be used to develop effective teams. Teams which are balanced, are open and confronting, whose members support and trust each other, who use co-operation and conflict wisely, who have sound procedures and appropriate leadership, who review to improve, who place a high priority on the development of members, have sound relations with other groups and have good communications are the ones most likely to succeed. The principal purpose of this book is to help you to take the strategic decisions which are necessary before teambuilding commences and to introduce you to the building blocks of effective teamwork.

If you decide to embark on teambuilding, you will probably want some practical help and advice on how to begin. There are many books and teambuilding strategies designed to help you. We have produced several which give practical advice and tools to carry out effective teambuilding interventions. They are:

TEAM DEVELOPMENT MANUAL (SECOND EDITION)

Mike Woodcock, Gower, 1989

Mike Woodcock's bestselling manual brings together basic theory, a diagnostic instrument, descriptions of the key elements of effective teamwork and a detailed guide to sources of further information and help, both in the UK and overseas. A particularly valuable feature is the 'building blocks' questionnaire that allows the manager or trainer to identify weaknesses in his or her team and to decide on appropriate action for overcoming them.

With its practical, down-to-earth approach, Team Development Manual appeals to managers in every type of organisation, as well as to personnel and training specialists and advisers.

CONTENTS

ACTIVITIES FOR TEAMBUILDING – A COMPANION VOLUME TO TEAM DEVELOPMENT MANUAL

Mike Woodcock, Connaught Training, 1988

A comprehensive collection of trainer-led activities for developing teambuilding skills. Each activity contains a statement of objectives and a full description, together with notes and variations. Many of them also include questionnaires, role-play briefs and other supporting documentation. The material is presented in the form of a looseleaf binder and carries the right to photocopy.

In addition to the activities the book contains an analysis of the building blocks of effective teamwork, a quick reference guide to help locate activities appropriate to particular problems, and a checklist for designing teambuilding events.

CONTENTS

Preface
1. Using the book
2. The building blocks of effective teamwork

THE ACTIVITIES

12. Brainstorming
13. Team openness exercise
14. Review and appraisal meetings
15. Enlivening meetings
16. How good a coach are you?
17. Being a better coach
18. Counselling to increase learning
19. Management style
20. Discussing values
21. Team member development needs
22. Who are you?
23. Intimacy exercise
24. Highway Code – a consensus-seeking activity
25. Is the team listening?
26. Cave rescue
27. Initial review
28. Prisoner's dilemma
29. The Zin obelisk
30. Clover leaf
31. Four-letter words
32. Team tasks
33. Making meetings more constructive
34. Positive and negative feedback
35. Improving one-to-one relationships
36. To see ourselves as others see us
37. Process review
38. How we make decisions
39. Team self-review
40. Silent shapes
41. Basic meeting arrangements
42. Decision-taking
43. Communication skills inventory
44. Team stock-take
45. My role in the team
46. Devising a team vision
47. Inter-group feedback
48. Burying the old team
49. Organisational types audit
50. Balancing team roles

FIFTY ACTIVITIES FOR UNBLOCKING YOUR ORGANISATION (VOLUMES 1 AND 2)

M. Woodcock and D. Francis, Connaught Training, 1990/1

These two volumes of structured activities devised by the authors are aimed principally at the organisational level.

However, many can be adapted for use on Team Development Programmes and the following are appropriate in their present published format. In each case the first number denotes the Volume and the second the Activity number.

1	13	The Extra Push
1	22	The Job as a Motivator
1	29	Microlab
1	32	Organisational Mirroring
1	44	Team Analysis
1	45	Team Leader's Review
2	4	Building a Team
2	10	Facilitator Skills Questionnaire
2	11	Group Video Analysis
2	13	Ice Breaker
2	15	Inter-Team Development
2	24	Motivating Environment Questionnaire
2	35	String Along
2	36	Teambuilding Competence Checklist
2	37	The Team Decision Making Questionnaire
2	38	Team Feedback
2	48	Work Group Climate Questionnaire
2	50	Yesterday's Good Idea

CHANGE

Francis and Woodcock, Connaught Training, 1992

Team development has at its heart the change process.

This collection of Activities and Exercises is intended to help the trainer and manager to prepare to manage change, to articulate choices, to vision the future and to implement change. Of particular relevance to the teambuilding process are the following structured activities and exercises contained in the volume:

1. Acquisitions Checklist
4. Club Fun
5. Decision Making Styles Review

6. The DIY Sheds Problem
7. Dynamic Firepower Corporation: A Case Study
8. Generating Strategic Options Checklist
12. Management Paradigms Questionnaire
14. The Mighty Mouse Organiser Company: A Case Study in Decision Making
15. Motivators at Work
17. Objective Setting Review
19. Organisational Options
20. Organisational Visioning
21. Practical Visioning
25. Strategic Failure: A Mini-Workshop

FIFTY ACTIVITIES FOR SELF DEVELOPMENT

Francis and Woodcock, Connaught Training, 1982

This volume is primarily directed at developing management and leadership skills and is then highly relevant to the development of team leaders. The following activities are particularly relevant for use in Teambuilding Programmes and in helping to improve teambuilding skills:

1. A Message To You
3. A Problem Solving Inventory
5. Blockages to Motivation
9. Counselling Skills Audit
11. Directing Others
14. Eggs Can Fly
19. Good Listening Habits
21. Highway Code
24. Individual or Team Decision?
28. Meetings Review
31. Process Review
35. The Working Day
37. Unlimited Adventure
38. Using Brainstorming
39. Using Creativity
46. Who is He?
49. Zen 1 – The Obelisk
50. Zen 2 – Isabela Monumento

TOP TEAM AUDIT

Dave Francis and Don Young, Gower, 1992

This practical kit designed by Dave Francis and Don Young is for facilitators who wish to work with strategy level teams. There are five components which build into a comprehensive process for top team development. The materials are provided ready to use on training programmes and workshops.

The components are:

1. Facilitator's Guide: gives step-by-step instructions to facilitate a top teambuilding process.
2. Top Team Review Survey: provides a structured framework for assessing top team effectiveness using 12 categories of effectiveness.
3. Top Team Roles Audit: clarifies the different contributions that top team members can make to the team.
4. Organisation Survey: defines the effectiveness of the top team through the eyes of the organisation's members.
5. Strategy Workbook: takes a top team through the process of defining the organisation's strategy.

Index

Action Profiling
Generating competitive edge through realizing management potential
Second Edition

Pamela Ramsden and Jody Zacharias

Much time and effort is wasted in organizations when managers work extremely hard but not in ways that are most productive for themselves or for others. This book describes a systematic approach to the study of managerial behaviour which can improve both personal performance and team and organizational effectiveness. The authors explain how a vast reservoir of hidden potential can be tapped when it is recognized that every manager has an individual pattern of driving forces. When this "Action Profile" pattern is observed and analysed, it can be used to increase productivity in key areas like decision making, gaining commitment to action and working across functional boundaries. The book shows how Action Profiling can help individuals optimize time and energy through a better use of their own and their colleagues' strengths, how errors can be reduced by recognizing and overcoming dangerous weaknesses and how management teams can combine decision analysis with enhanced motivation to achieve improved results with less effort. The text is supported by numerous illustrations and by detailed accounts of successful applications in companies as diverse as Hewlett Packard, ICI and Kodak. The Action Profile system offers individual managers helpful insights into their strengths and weaknesses and also provides organizations with an objective basis for recruitment, motivation, team development and improved decision analysis and problem solving.

1993   404 pages   0 566 02727 5

Gower

Building a Better Team
A handbook for
managers and facilitators

Peter Moxon

Team leadership and team development are central to the modern manager's ability to "achieve results through other people". Successful team building requires knowledge and skill, and the aim of this handbook is to provide both. Using a unique blend of concepts, practical guidance and exercises, the author explains both the why and the how of team development.

Drawing on his extensive experience as manager and consultant, Peter Moxon describes how groups develop, how trust and openness can be encouraged, and the likely problems overcome. As well as detailed advice on the planning and running of teambuilding programmes the book contains a series of activities, each one including all necessary instructions and support material.

Irrespective of the size or type of organization involved, <u>Building a Better Team</u> offers a practical, comprehensive guide to managers, facilitators and team leaders seeking improved performance.

Contents

1993   208 pages   0 566 07424 9

Gower

Empowering People at Work

Nancy Foy

This is a book written, says the author, "for the benefit of practical managers coping with real people in real organizations". Part I shows how the elements of empowerment work together: performance focus, teams, leadership and face-to-face communication. Part II explains how to manage the process of empowerment, even in a climate of "downsizing" and "delayering". It includes chapters on networking, listening, running effective team meetings, giving feedback, training and using employee surveys. Part III contains case studies of IBM and British Telecom and examines the way they have developed employee communication to help achieve corporate objectives.

The final section comprises a review of communication channels that can be used to enhance the empowerment process, an extensive set of survey questions to be selected on a "pick and mix" basis and an annotated guide to further reading.

Empowerment is probably the most important concept in the world of management today, and Nancy Foy's new book will go a long way towards helping managers to "make it happen".

Contents

1994   288 pages   0 566 07436 2

Gower

Gower Handbook of Training and Development
Second Edition

Edited by John Prior MBE

This Gower Handbook, published in association with the Institute of Training & Development, first appeared in 1991 and quickly established itself as a standard work. For this new edition the text has been completely revised to reflect recent developments and new chapters have been added on cultural diversity, learning styles and choosing resources. The Handbook now contains contributions from no fewer than forty nine experienced professionals, each one an expert in his or her chosen subject.

For anyone involved in training and development, whether in business or the public sector, the Handbook represents an unrivalled resource.

Contents

1994   640 pages   0 566 07446 X

How Managers Can Develop Managers

Alan Mumford

Managers are constantly being told that they are responsible for developing other managers. This challenging book explains why and how this should be done.

Moving beyond the familiar territory of appraisal, coaching and courses, Professor Mumford examines ways of using day-to-day contact to develop managers. The emphasis is on learning from experience - from the job itself, from problems and opportunities, from bosses, mentors and colleagues.

Among the topics covered are:
- recognizing learning opportunities
- understanding the learning process
- what being helped involves
- the skills required to develop others
- the idea of reciprocity ("I help you, you help me")

Throughout the text there are exercises designed to connect the reader's own experience to the author's ideas. The result is a powerful and innovative work from one of Europe's foremost writers on management development.

Contents

Introduction • Part I: How Managers Learn • What managers do • Management and learning • Opportunities for learning • The learning process • Part II: The Art and Craft of Developing Managers • Ways of helping • The helping relationship • Helping individuals to learn • Learning in groups • Formal development for individuals • Formal development for groups • How to be helped • Develop yourself • Towards the learning organization • Appendix: The role of the professional adviser • Index.

1993   240 pages   0 566 07403 6

Gower

A Manual for Change

Terry Wilson

Change is now the only constant, as the cliché has it, and organizations who fail to master change are likely to find themselves undone by it.

In this unique manual, Terry Wilson provides the tools for planning and implementing a systematic organizational change programme. The first section enables the user to determine the scope and scale of the programme. Next, a change profile is completed based on twelve key factors. Finally, each of the factors is reviewed in the context of the user's own organization. Questionnaries and exercises are provided throughout and any manager working through these will have not only a clear understanding of the change process but also specific plans ready to put into action.

Derived from the author's experience of working with organizations at every level and in a wide range of industries, the manual will be invaluable to directors, managers, consultants and professional trainers battling to help their organizations survive and flourish in an increasingly turbulent environment.

Contents

Using this manual • Change programme focus: The scale of change • Change process profile: The twelve factors • Factor one Perspectives: Maintaining the overall view • Factor two The change champion: Leading the change • Factor three The nature of change: Identifying the change affecting us • Factor four Unified management vision: Importance of management agreement • Factor five Change of organizational philosophy: Modernizing the organization • Factor six Change phases: Four phases of change • Factor seven The 10/90 rule: Vision and real change • Factor eight Transitional management: Management role and style • Factor nine Teamwork: Importance of teams • Factor ten Changing behaviour: Identifying the critical factors • Factor eleven Expertise and resources: Assessing requirements • Factor twelve Dangers and pitfalls: Planning to avoid difficulties.

1994   191 pages   0 566 07460 5

Gower